QUEEN OF FREEDOM

DEFENDING JAMAICA

HOW QUEEN NANNY

Catherine Johnson, Fellow of the Royal Society of Literature, is an award-winning children's author with over 20 novels to her name. Her love of storytelling began at home, where both of her parents were great storytellers. She loves to write about the people that aren't seen often in regular history and has written many books for younger readers with a historical setting. These include *Sawbones*, a murder mystery set in eighteenth-century London, and *The Curious Tale of the Lady Caraboo*, about a cobbler's daughter from Devon who, in the early nineteenth-century, passed herself off as a princess of Indonesia. A Londoner by birth, Catherine is half-Jamaican and has visited the Blue Mountains, where Queen Nanny lived with her people.

QUEEN OF FREEDOM

DEFENDING JAMAICA

CATHERINE JOHNSON

With illustrations by Amerigo Pinelli

PUSHKIN CHILDREN'S

WEST NORTHAMPTONSHIRE COUNCIL	
60000475210	
Askews & Holts	
ND	

Pushkin Press
71–75 Shelton Street
London WC2H 9JQ

First published in the UK by Pushkin Press in 2020

1 3 5 7 9 8 6 4 2

ISBN 13: 978-1-78269-279-9

Designed and typeset by Tetragon, London
Printed and bound by CPI Group (UK) Ltd, Croydon, CRO 4YY

www.pushkinpress.com

QUEEN OF FREEDOM

Jamaica 1720s

Jamaica Channel

Montego Bay

Cockpit Country

LEEWARD MAROONS
Accompang Town

Bagnall's
Thicket

Annotto Bay

Albany

new Nanny Town
old Nanny Town

WINDWARD MAROONS

Blue Mountains

Kingston

Quao Hill

Caribbean Sea

1720

WINDWARD JAMAICA

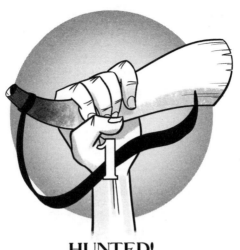

HUNTED!

In the Blue Mountains,
Parish of St George

The raid had been a mistake. The redcoats were after them, crashing through the trees and undergrowth.

The cows Quao and Johnny Rain Bird had stolen would be useful, but not if they all ended up dead. Nanny told the men to go east and circle back to town; she and Yaw and the pig – Michele – would go west.

But she had been running for so long and the redcoats were still coming. The thorns cut her feet, tore at the skin on her legs, and vines whipped her onwards. Behind her the soldiers snapped branches,

9

shouted threats. Birds flew up, calling, yelling. As she ran, the cutlass – as long as her thigh – slapped and bounced against her leg.

The boy and the pig galloped ahead.

She had been hunted before. So had Yaw. The times she thought she had escaped, only to be dragged back, punished with shackles and chains and beatings. She would not let them catch her now. She would never go back to the cane fields, to the lash and the overseer and the buckra. Never. And she had responsibilities now, to the village, to her new family. She should never have agreed to taking the pig with Yaw. Had she ever been a child? She could not remember.

Yaw looked back at her, grinning. This was all still a game to him. Her heart was beating so hard and so fast she thought it might leap out of her chest.

'Run, Yaw!' she called.

Then a sharp crack-crack. She thought it was a branch, at first, breaking. Then another, a hard, dry snapping noise. Then another sound, a whirring – a bird, a hornet? No, something else cut the air past her face.

Bullets. They were shooting at them.

Another whistled past. Her skin stung: it had grazed her, made a red line across her upper arm.

They would kill them both. She heard them reload. Up in the trees a monkey screamed.

'Yaw!' she yelled. 'Faster!'

'Stop! In the name of the King!' The soldier's voice bounced off the leaves and the hills.

She had caught up with the boy now. The pig, head down, was almost pulling him along.

'They cannot catch us, Nanny,' Yaw said. 'The gods are on our side! We stole Michele and we will take her home. We will—'

Another crack-crack-crack and Yaw pulled up, stock-still. Then, as the world stopped, he crumpled to the ground and Nanny watched open-mouthed as he folded in on himself in the way the shamey plant leaves curl up when you step on them. A red flower bloomed above his temple and his eyes turned up inside his head.

Nanny reached him as he let go of both the rope and the pig, his hand loose, his fingers useless. Michele stopped too; she snorted, her white flanks heaving. Nanny halted, bent over Yaw's body as another volley of bullets cut through the air right where her head had just been.

'Yaw!' Nanny cried out. She felt his pain like a blow to her chest.

She looked up and could see the flashes of red and gold where the soldiers moved between the trees. She knew she was next.

She gathered him up in her arms. The charms he wore on a string in a tiny cloth bag around his neck

hung loose. His head was all meat now. The soldiers were closer.

Nanny blinked; her hands were wet with sweat and Yaw's blood. She had to put him down but she whispered into his one whole ear, 'I will not leave you, Yaw.'

Then before the redcoats came any closer, she wiped her palms on her plaid cotton dress and shinned up a soursop tree. Clinging and flattening herself on a branch directly above the body of Yaw – lying on the forest floor, one eye ruined, one staring up at the blue sky – she shut her eyes and tried to imagine his spirit floating past and flying home across the wide ocean.

Michele, the pig, stayed close, nudging Yaw as if he might get up if only he had some encouragement.

Then suddenly the soldiers were upon him. Four men burst upon the track like monsters, pink and red-and-white and gold, their whiskers bristling, their weapons dark. They smelled of gunpowder and sweat and death.

One kicked the boy as if he were nothing. Michele squealed and went for the red-faced soldier before running off into the bush. Another cursed and aimed for the pig with his gun, but Nanny was pleased to note Michele was too fast.

The tallest soldier bent over Yaw and pulled his shirt down off his shoulder.

'He's one of the Fairview slaves,' he said. 'From over Mount Vernon. There's the mark there, Captain Shettlewood.'

Yaw's shoulder bore a lumpy raised scar. Nanny blinked. She remembered the pain when the hot iron had seared those same letters and the shape of a heart onto her own skin.

'Good shooting, Geoffrey,' the redcoat called Shettlewood noted. 'Only a few more to round up, although Mr Noach would rather have all the property returned alive.'

'Yes, sir.' The soldier tried to click to attention. 'Pig's alive, though.'

'Lost in the bush?' The captain poked at Yaw with his foot. 'That animal's as good as dead.'

'What should we do with him? The boy?' The soldier wiped the sweat off his face.

'Leave him,' the captain said, bending over Yaw's body. 'The ants will soon eat out his eyes. A warning to the others. We'll find her soon enough too.'

The soldiers looked around the clearing as if willing her to appear. Nanny put her hand on the hilt of her cutlass. But there were too many of them...

'When the reinforcements arrive, Private Geoffrey' – the captain said, standing up – 'we will wipe those Maroons from the face of the earth. We know their village can't be more than a few miles from here. It's only a matter of time.'

'Yes, sir!'

Nanny wished she had a gun. She wished she could rain down all the worst things on those men's heads. She prayed to bring down the shit of every bird, the vomit of all the monkeys. She stared. She sent all the hatred that flooded through her body down onto those soldiers.

As the men walked away, Nanny saw one of them slip, heard him curse with pain as his knee turned over. Perhaps it was Obeah, the old magic? Perhaps the gods had not forgotten them after all.

She felt the anger rise inside: if they *were* here, then why was Yaw dead?

When she was sure they had gone she carefully inched down the soursop tree, almost holding her breath just in case the soldiers were still there. Then she heaved the small boy's body across her shoulders and disappeared into the bush along the faint whisper of a track the soldiers had not seen.

It was hard going, running and hiding through the bush with Yaw's body on her back. When she reached their makeshift village, Nanny laid the little boy down outside his hut. She took the old cow horn trumpet, the abeng that hung from the hog-apple tree and blew as hard and as long as she could.

First Efua and Helen came out from the gardens where they were tending sorrel and callaloo, then Johnny Rain Bird and Quao came from the forest where they were cutting wood to make a pen for the cows. Soon the whole town was there. There were some tears when they saw Yaw lying still and dead, but most of her fellow Coromantees had seen suffering of one kind or another.

'It was redcoats, from the fort at Bagnall's Thicket.' Nanny looked out at the faces of her comrades. Some of the little children were still weeping. 'Now he is free.' It felt like a lie. He was not *free*. He was *dead* and gone. She took a breath. 'It should not have been. I should have stopped him. I should not have encouraged him.'

'None of us stopped him,' Quao said. 'Yaw would have gone back for that pig on his own if he could have.'

Efua began to sing – a sad song from home that Nanny knew. All the town joined in, sending the song up into the air, chasing Yaw's young spirit back across the ocean.

When the song finished Nanny spoke again. 'There will be no more raids for pigs. I learned one thing from the soldiers. More are coming. They want to destroy us. To wipe this town, our town, from the face of the earth.'

Someone in the crowd shouted, 'No!'

There were more shouts and stamps.

Nanny put her arms out for quiet.

'We must work hard,' she said. 'They will have men. And guns.' She held up Yaw's gris gris: the charms he had worn around his neck. 'These will not protect us alone. We need guns and cutlasses too.' She looked over her fellows, each one, she knew, willing to give their blood to live free. 'And most important, we must know when they come before they put a foot on our mountain. We must cut the buckra down before they take us and break our backs.'

Then the drum beat and the abeng blew out a final farewell to Yaw. Nanny bent down and took the hand knife the boy had kept at his belt and tied it onto her own, then she whispered into his good ear, 'I will never forget you. As long as I wear your knife at my belt, you are with me.'

Then the singing began again and Nanny returned Yaw's body to sleep in the red earth.

A CLEVER WOMAN

The only one in the Maroon village who'd seen the soldiers' camp at Bagnall's Thicket was Quao. 'I dig redcoats' latrines for a week,' he said. 'Them have outbreak of flux down there. Smelled like hell come out of them mans' bowels straight down into the earth.'

'You seen how many of them were there?' Nanny asked.

Quao shrugged. 'More than countable.'

Nanny sighed. 'We have to find out. We have to be prepared.' She would have to take him with her.

Nanny knew the place was on the far side of Albany, a town along the trail that led from Kingston in the south to the sea at Port Antonio in the north. It was a place where local people came down once a week to sell produce, and where the local plantation owners stopped to see the occasional coffle of slaves fresh come off the boat. So this morning, a market day in September time, the two of them made their way down from the village in the mountains towards town. The tracks were hard to find – the bush grew so fast and so strong, it kept the village hidden. Even though the island was a place – mostly – of death and sorrow, everything was so alive, so green and vital. As they came to the river, the whirlpool at the foot of the waterfall glittered and shone.

'We best not cross too near,' Quao said. 'I seen a calf pull down to die in there one time.'

Nanny nodded. She remembered that too. She wondered about Michele, Yaw's pig, and hoped for the best.

Once they reached the main road Quao was uncomfortable, dragging his feet like he was a little boy and not a grown man. He had on his good shirt and carried a basket of guinep and pawpaw. He stopped to shift the load and felt for his gris gris, the charm of herbs and ground-up bones he wore around his neck.

'Why we bother come this way?' he said. 'You know I don't like coming into town, plenty of people know me from the plantation up Mount Vernon, see me, steal me back.'

Nanny carried her basket of fruit on her head. She was uncomfortable too: wearing the wide, full skirts in the English style meant her cutlass thump thumped against her leg as she walked.

'Hush up, Quao,' she scolded him. 'Keep your head down and your ears open. How we going to find out how many redcoats they have if we don't look with our own eyes?' She wished she had taken Johnny Rain Bird or Mary or Hester Jane with her instead.

Quao went on, 'I don't see why I couldn't have gone to the Thicket while you in the market. Save time.'

'I need you. We look like farmers, come down from the hills. Free people. And we need some buckets, and iron nails for fixing up tools. And Hester say she need some good twine, not the home-made kind. I can't carry everything on my own.'

Quao kissed the charm and muttered a prayer to the old gods.

Nanny had been thinking about Obeah since Yaw's death. 'Sometimes I reckon those old gods shut up their ears. If they were listening, do you think any of us would be here? So far from home? Scratching a living and hiding from folk who want to kill us or worse!'

Quao tucked the charms away. 'Obeah is powerful magic!' he said, his voice low. Nanny rolled her eyes. 'And is a comfort, Nanny.'

Nanny kept walking. She sighed. She wished there was more of a comfort in the old gods for her. Instead she thought of her cutlass and, tucked inside her cotton skirts, Yaw's knife, small and sharp and ready. 'Only comfort for me is the edge of my blade,' she said grimly.

It was still early when they found themselves out of the forest and down from the mountains on the track just outside Albany. The sun was up but the heat wasn't burning yet, even though the moisture in the air made it heavy going.

In the small square in the centre of town some of the locals were already setting out their wares on banana leaves or on mats. Men and women, all shades from yellow to ink dark, spread out oranges and almonds, bananas and breadfruit, plantain and okra. There was even an old straggle-haired white man with some goats tethered to a post.

Nanny and Quao set out their produce. Quao pulled his old straw hat down over one eye. 'Just in case buckra from Mount Vernon hop into town to buy some goat,' he said.

From across the square a tall woman carried four chickens, two in each hand. They dangled by their feet, wings out, scarcely flapping. They knew their fate. Nanny nodded at her: she and Ophelia went back a long time. Ophelia had bought her own freedom when the old white man who kept her as his wife died, and now she lived up in the mountains towards Bog Walk. She was dressed all in white this morning, from the scarf wrapped round her hair, to the skirt that grazed the ground at her feet.

Nanny nodded hello. 'That's Ophelia,' she said to Quao. 'I know her a long time. She always a help to me.'

Quao turned to look. 'Ophelia? She have strong Obeah, I heard. She can talk to plant and tree and rock.'

Nanny laughed. 'Obeah?' She shook her head. 'She simply clever,' Nanny said. 'That's all. Cleverer than the whitest Englishman that ever live. Once her husband die and she live alone, she had to find a way to get people to leave her be. She tell stories. And she tell them so people want to believe them.'

Quao huffed. 'It Obeah. I heard it, seen it…'

Nanny didn't argue. She had believed it all once. But since Yaw had died…

It was a few hours later, close to noon, Nanny reckoned from the angle of the sun, when two white men – one with an expensive yellow straw hat, one with a long gun – came into the square leading a coffle of slaves.

Five men, one woman, all, yoked together and shuffling. The saddest kind of dance, Nanny thought. Then behind them, not tall enough to fit in the yoke, two small boys, one tinier than Yaw, his belly stretched round – not with food, Nanny knew, but with hunger. They were all shining, the oil rubbed into their skin to make them look healthy. Their eyes all empty, like walking dead folk.

It was as if a cold wind blew into town. The market folk quietened.

Nanny wanted to look away but she couldn't. Suddenly she remembered the smell of the ship. The bodies and the shit and the slap slap of the water against the wooden walls. She looked at Quao and knew he was thinking the same thing.

In the square, the white man with the gun turned a barrel over and unfastened the yoke. The tallest slave, long, long legs, straightened up under the relief of being yoked to his shorter comrades. His face, like theirs, impassive, carved in stone, still with sadness. They had forgotten everything, anything but pain. Nanny blinked, remembering. The children betrayed their fear with the slightest trembling around the mouth.

For a second Nanny thought the tall man saw her. Then she looked away, ashamed for looking. Ashamed for everything he had lost. Ashamed he was here and she could do nothing for him. She sent her thoughts to him. To all of them. Something else was possible. Another life. Was possible. She wished wished wished the Obeah Quao held faith in was real.

One of the children wailed. The spell was broken.

The square was filling up with white people. Mostly men, in good straw hats, and mostly in coats even though the sun was high now. Their faces were red rather than white, and shining damp, or in some cases running wet with sweat. Several held cotton handkerchiefs to their foreheads or dabbed them about the skin at the back of their necks.

Nanny saw Quao freeze. He was staring at one tall white man with a battered hat and a long rifle of his own.

'Is Michael Noach,' he said low. 'Overseer from Mount Vernon.' Quao pulled his hat low as he could. 'I told you,' he hissed urgently. 'I told you so!'

'We go,' Nanny agreed. 'Forget the twine. Bucket can wait.'

Across the square Nanny saw Ophelia approach with two of the chickens – she must have sold the others – and make her way towards her. She pointed at the produce. For a second Nanny wondered how she knew what was happening and whether anyone else did.

Ophelia handed over the chickens to Nanny. 'I take over here,' she said. Nanny nodded. Ophelia untied something from around her neck and placed it around Nanny's, tucking it inside the top of her dress. It was one of her own charms, tied with a bright blue cord. 'Go,' she said.

Nanny wanted to protest, but knew the woman meant well.

Quao started through the crowd and Nanny followed him, the chickens making no sound. She felt for Yaw's knife and wrapped her hand tight around it

She looked behind her one last time. One of the slavers was calling out to the crowd and indicating the long-legged, dark-skinned man. 'See this? Fine Coromantee buck, fresh from the boat, fine and strong! Will make back his price in weeks!' The white man pulled back the man's gums. 'We call him Caesar – as ain't he just an emperor among his fellows! Good teeth, no flux. What am I bid?'

The tall man pulled his mouth away. He cried out, 'My name is Adou!'

Nanny turned away before she heard the blow that came, the sound of stick meeting flesh.

She shut her ears and set her eyes for the road to Bagnall's Thicket, her cutlass swinging, her eyes prickling with heat and fury. She turned back for one last look at the tall young man, dark skin, his jaw set hard against the whole world. Nanny wished the old gods were here with her now. With him. She wished they were more than simply stories and dreams.

She hurried to catch up to Quao.

It was less than a quarter mile to the army camp. They heard it before they saw it, the sound of sawing, of trees felling. Quao slowed.

'They building, Nanny,' he said. 'Making room for more of themselves.'

Nanny fell into step. The track was still wide enough for a horse and cart, and they could both tell from the ruts in the earth that the recent traffic had been heavy.

'We can't go much farther,' Quao said. 'Path here passes by but narrows. We have to turn back, or walk a mile and a mile – long way home.'

'Then that is what we do,' Nanny said. And the chickens flapped their agreement.

Quao sighed and they walked on.

Suddenly the tree cover was gone and they were walking on the edge of a clearing filled with houses made of what looked like the same sort of canvas as they used for the sails of their ships.

'Them tents,' Quao said. 'And there are more of them than before. A whole new field of houses the redcoats made. Seen?'

Nanny did see. The smell was of cut logs and unwashed men. It made Nanny think of the ship more than anything.

'Latrine,' Quao said. 'It full now.' His lip curled.

Nanny tried to scan the camp. 'How many more come?' she asked. 'Since you were here?'

They walked slowly along the road, snatching glances and looks.

Quao whistled. 'Numbers are not my strongest suit.'

'Twice as many then?'

So many men buzzed around the camp like red ants. There were some in coats, some bare-chested, wrestling, some sawing wood, some washing down horses.

Quao looked once more. 'I reckon it three times. There are more tents and more stables and those guns on wheels that fire cannonball.'

'They busy.' Nanny put her hand to the small knife, to give her strength.

Quao looked at her. 'You think that man, Captain Shettlewood, him in there right now?'

Nanny shrugged. 'Perhaps. The captains have the white wigs under their hats.'

Quao shook his head. 'Why do they do that? Cut off their hair and wear someone else's own? Does it protect them? Do you think they have charms woven in the hair? Good luck? Spells to kill us?'

Nanny kept walking. 'You think they die of heat. Maybe they cold.'

Quao nodded. 'They have no heart.'

'I'm not so sure, Quao,' Nanny said. She lifted the chickens into her other hand. 'They all just the same as us. They choose to act the way they do. They have hearts, every man and woman of them, they just choose not to listen to theirs.'

They reached the far side of the camp before they turned back towards the mountains. As they did so, they saw redcoats wheeling out three more of the massive cannons.

Quao walked faster. 'How we fight that?' He put his hand up to the charms around his neck. 'Those guns blast the whole town. They kill us all.' Quao looked at her. 'We better go west – I hear Cudjoe have more people than us, more fighters than us, over in Cockpit Country.'

Nanny kept walking. 'We not going anywhere. We will fight them. How can they pull those heavy guns up the mountain? Through the bush and trees? We can stop them before they five miles away.'

'How? More of them arrive every day and every man jack of them have a rifle! We cannot win, Nanny. Not without Obeah, without magic.'

Nanny smiled. 'We cannot rely on prayers. Don't we know that? We need something more, we need to be clever.' She swung the chickens up over her back. 'Just like Ophelia.'

MAKING STORIES COME TRUE

Free Windward Maroon Town, Blue Mountains

I t was afternoon, the heat of the day had begun to cool, and the men and women and children had done with tending their crops of callaloo and okra. Nanny stood in the open space in front of the huts, leaning on her cutlass.

On the other side of the clearing was Quao. He was wearing a jacket taken a long long time ago from a dead English soldier, all faded red and gold braid. He was taller than Nanny and broader than her, and behind him stood at least half the town.

'We wait till the corn ripe,' he said. 'Carry everything west, start again in a new town with

Cudjoe's people. We not strong enough to resist the redcoat.' He looked out across the people. 'I seen how many come. I went into town and saw with my own eyes the men, the guns.'

There was a ripple of agreement.

Nanny shifted. 'And how long, tell me, till the corn ready?' she asked. 'And the pumpkin?'

Hester Jane steadied the baby on her hip. 'Maybe three week?'

'Mine a little longer,' Johnny Rain Bird added.

'So what if them redcoats come sooner?' Nanny said. 'Who wants to leave the crops we work hard hard at for last months, year? What if they come tomorrow or the day after or the day after that? We have to fight and be prepared. And we can fight! Not out in the open, the way they do, ready aim fire!' Nanny mimed a rifle on her shoulder. She paused, looked hard at Johnny. 'We must use the bush, the trees, the streams.'

Some of the people looked interested.

Hester looked at Nanny, 'I work hard hard clearing that ground.'

'But how streams save us from bullets?' Quao said. His hand went up to the gris gris around his neck. 'The gods say—'

Nanny cut him off. 'The gods? They whisper in your ear at night? Only whispers I hear is the sounds of my mother and brothers die on the boat. They all tell me to stand up, and Yaw, gone last week, he would want us to fight.'

There were more nods from the crowd and Nanny went on. 'We know every rock, every tree, every trail, every bend in the river, every waterfall, whirlpool. These redcoats, most of them fresh off the boat, most of them never heard the sound of our birds, of our trees in the wind. We can be like duppy, like ghosts, we can make them fear us.' She looked across the group. 'We can win.'

More nods. Nanny looked around.

Quao frowned.

Nanny took her cutlass and drew in the dirt. 'This the river, this the town, this the mountain track. We keep lookouts day and night. We set up ambush on the trail, here and here. And Quao? Remember that calf in the whirlpool?'

Quao cut his eyes at her. 'You think we throw them in the river?! There are too many—'

'Not all of them. Enough to scare the life out of their hearts,' Nanny said. And she could feel Hester and Johnny Rain Bird and all the other villagers listening hard. They could see how it could be.

She went on, 'We make them think all the stories about ghosts, about spirits, are true. We make them believe all the Obeah stories they hear down in town are the truth.' Nanny felt she had them on her side now. 'And we make every one of those stories come true-true.'

Quao looked at her. 'I still think we leave, go Leeward, to Cudjoe…'

Nanny looked straight at him, nodded. 'If you want, you go. I say we make ready, and if then, if people want to leave when the crops done, they go, we all go maybe. After all, we are free. No one make any of us do what we don't want to do.'

There was a chorus of agreement. She looked at Quao. There was a long pause, then he nodded too. She put out her hand to shake his and for a moment she thought he might not take it.

'We work together, Quao,' she said. And, at last, he took it.

They posted lookouts that evening. There were only two abeng – shell trumpets – but Johnny Rain Bird did a good whistler call, and another could make a fair mockingbird. Nanny agreed bird calls were probably better than trumpets.

Then Nanny and a working party went down to the trail that led up from Albany and cut trees to block the track. Another party went down to the river and made sure to hide the shallow crossing place, by moving some of the smaller rocks and digging out the bank. A third party diverted the trail along narrower paths where horses and cannon could not pass. And if the soldiers came one by one, then it would be easier and simpler to pick them off. Vital, given the whole village had only two working rifles and one handgun.

Then, and just as importantly, she and the townsfolk strung bird and animal bones along the paths. A large caiman skull was fixed to a tall meroe tree and Nanny herself spatchcocked the body of a dead monkey that she had found on the path. It was a horrible thing, she thought, arms and legs open as if wanting to embrace the world, yet in fact dead and rotten. As she pinned the monkey to the frame, she spoke to it inside her head. Its spirit would not be happy, she knew that, and she was sorry for it.

Some of the children built up piles of stinking herbs ready to burn – the ones that smelled like hell, even though they did nothing.

Nanny tried the path out herself. The bush was close here, and even at noon with the sun at its height it was cool and the dappled light made everything move and swim a little. Hester had suggested drums – a good drumbeat that told the redcoats they were not afraid, and that might take the English in the wrong direction. Drums and bones and herbs. Would it be enough?

On the fourth day when the redcoats still had not come, Nanny went down into Albany to see Ophelia.

Ophelia lived in a cottage on the western edge of the town where the trees started coming in from the mountain. She kept goats and chickens and tended her garden.

Nanny found her on her verandah, drying herbs. She took off the borrowed charms and folded the little bag back into Ophelia's hand.

'I thank you for the chickens, Miss Ophelia, and while I return your good luck I come to ask your help.'

Ophelia sat back in her chair.

'We need you to spread some stories,' Nanny said.

'That easy enough.'

'And we need to trade for guns.' Nanny sat down. 'We have three in all, and redcoats have cannon and rifle and enough shot and powder to kill us all three times over.'

Ophelia raised an eyebrow. Her face said that would not be easy at all.

'At least you are not laughing,' Nanny said.

'I can't help you with guns. I hear up Mount Vernon they have plenty of rifle, but locked away.' Ophelia shrugged. 'But the stories,' she said, sitting back in her chair, 'I can make them as powerful as ten cannonball, set them off and explode them straight inside that army camp.'

Nanny smiled.

'One thing.' Ophelia gave the charms back to Nanny. 'You be needing these. Make sure everyone see them.' She gave Nanny one look up and down. 'And find some more cutlass to wear at your waist. If they want a monster with all the power of Obeah, you give them one.' She took Nanny's hand and looked into her eyes. 'You be one. You be the thing that strike terror and fear into their heart. You ever kill a man?' she asked.

Nanny shook her head.

'Taking a life is easy.' Ophelia sat back in her cane chair. 'It's afterwards can be hard. You must be strong. You must know when to stop,' she said.

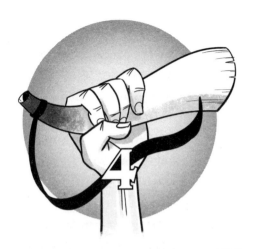

REDCOATS IN THE RIVER

Blue Mountains

They came three days after that. The alarm
worked. One of the children who'd been
among Yaw's playmates – a girl called
Meggy – came crashing into the village out of
breath.

'The redcoats!' she puffed. 'They starting up the
trail from Albany!' The little girl sucked in a mouthful
of air. 'They on their way!'

'You stay here now!' Nanny said, tying on her
cutlass. 'Take the other small ones and stay inside.'

Meggy nodded, eyes wide, and Nanny marshalled
the villagers, standing on a stool so they could all see
her.

Quao was loading his handgun, and tying on the horn that held his gunpowder. 'How we know if the stories have worked?' he said, not looking at her.

'We have to trust,' Nanny said.

Quao cocked the gun, eye squinting as if aiming. 'Trust,' he snorted, and for a second Nanny wasn't certain if he might not shoot her.

She swallowed. Moved the gun away as if he were nothing, as if he could never hurt her with anything.

'Start the drums when you hear the signal,' she said as if he was not there. 'We all know the plan. Hester, Johnny Rain Bird, stand in the clearing, lead them down the wrong path. Then Efua and Kwame, pop up at the head of the river, lead the redcoats just where we want them.'

Everyone nodded, serious.

'That way,' Nanny said, 'we herd them toward the river. Twos and threes, everyone! No talking. If you see the man, the Captain Shettlewood, you leave him for me!'

As she rushed down the bush trail she felt her good cutlass swinging, crashing against the two wooden ones she wore at her waist.

Her heart was thumping and she knew her companions felt the same; Hester's eyes were popping and Johnny Rain Bird held his bow so tight in his hand his knuckles practically burst out through his skin.

They reached their ambush point and hid behind a rock, just as the warning bird calls echoed through the bush. But they didn't need them as some of the English men were singing loudly – almost drunkenly. Not a bad tune, Nanny thought, though their voices were coarse and the words when she could make out what they were saying were coarser still.

'We herding goats toward the whirlpool,' Nanny whispered to her companions. 'Remember.'

Johnny Rain Bird and Hester nodded.

And then they came, the soldiers, stumbling through the trees, their red coats like points of light that would, Nanny hoped, guide Hester's arrows and, perhaps, Quao's bullets. The trail was narrow and they could only walk in single file. All the better to pick them off, Nanny knew.

'Make it to the river, boys!' The leader of this troop was not Shettlewood. He was younger, and he did not have a white wig. Nanny felt disappointed.

There was some grumbling from the soldiers. They looked hot and sweat ran down their faces.

'Then we can fill the canteens!' their leader barked.

The soldiers snaked their way down through the bush. The man in the front had a long shiny rifle. Fixed to the end of it was a silver blade – Nanny did not think she had ever seen the like.

'Mother of God!' The soldier at the front had come across the dead monkey. 'These people!'

The redcoat in charge came up alongside him, with difficulty though, as the path was so narrow. Nanny could not see his face but the tone of his voice told her everything.

'They are devils!' he said. Nanny was certain there was a slight tremble in his voice. 'Witches. No one is to be spared.'

The men behind were uneasy. She could hear it in the way they moved. Then the drums started up, a heavy insistent tolling sound, and the men at the back hurried to keep up with their leaders. Towards the river.

Nanny and her band followed, secretly, noiselessly, through the trees.

The redcoats relaxed as they reached the riverside. In a few minutes they had been joined by another group, and this time Nanny saw the white wig and the gold braid of Captain Shettlewood. Some of the soldiers had put down their weapons and their packs and pulled off their boots.

Nanny signalled with bird calls to wait. The more of the redcoats went in the water the better.

Nanny hoped the chiggers in the river could do some of the Maroons' work. She whispered to them, and hoped those tiny creatures heard the redcoats splashing and felt the heat off their bodies and swam close-close before boring into their skin to leave their eggs inside the redcoats' feet.

'We going to leave them?' Hester Jane whispered, watching.

'We going to kill them,' Nanny said. 'Leave them one or two to tell our tale.'

Suddenly a shout, and there, breaking cover from the far bank, was Yaw's little pig, Michele. She was here! Nanny took that as a good sign. One of the soldiers saw and raised his gun. Nanny motioned to Hester and whistled. Hester's first shot whirred through the air and hit the would-be pig killer square in the chest. Then a volley of arrows and the riverside suddenly was all confusion, shouting and splashing. The crack-crack of guns, and the river began to run red.

'Return fire!' That was Shettlewood. 'Return fire!'

But some of the soldiers had merely struck out for the far bank, and others slipped and fell in the rushing water, the whirlpool scooping them up and dragging them down.

On the far bank Quao was waiting with his handgun, and not one redcoat made it out of the water that way. They fell, like some kind of dance, Nanny thought.

Shettlewood was standing in the river sheltering behind a rock, long and lean with his rifle on his shoulder, firing wildly into the trees.

Nanny whistled again, high and clear, and the drums came louder, muffled and heavy like a thousand feet trampling out the redcoats' souls.

Then Nanny jumped out of the bush, her cutlass in her two hands, cutting down soldiers left and right. She heard bullets, she thought: one time the sound was so loud and so sharp, perhaps she was dead, and this person slashing out at arms and legs and thighs was a kind of zombie, a duppy, not made of flesh and bone but of hate and hurt.

The redcoats – those still alive – were scrambling for the banks, abandoning their weapons and running for the trees.

Shettlewood slipped and Nanny caught hold of him by his jacket. She swung at him, her cutlass sharper than any thought, and she felt the muscles in his arm sever. His mouth was open, crying out.

'This for Yaw,' she said as she let him go and he dropped to his feet in the river. Before she could think, she swung again and released his head, making it fly from his body and up and out into the steaming red water.

NOTHING STRONGER
THAN NANNY

Nanny Town, Blue Mountains

The victory celebrations went on for a night and a day. Hester Jane killed three of her chickens and the children fetched ripe mango and spiny soursop, plantain and custard apple, for the feast. They even killed one of the cows they had captured in the last raid.

There was some home-brewed mountain rum that tasted harsh against her throat, that Nanny felt burn her insides, but it made everyone merry and that warmed her heart.

Even Quao danced and danced, wearing his brand-new scarlet coat that he'd taken from one of the soldiers.

He whirled round so the tails flew up and out, until he was so tired he fell asleep with his arms around Michele, Yaw's pig, who had followed them all home from the fighting.

It was Johnny Rain Bird who had the idea. 'We name our town, this town, Nanny Town!' Everyone who was still awake agreed.

Nanny shook her head. 'It was all of us who sent those redcoats to hell, or back to Albany.'

'But the plan was yours,' Hester said, looking at Quao snuffling in his sleep. 'If we listen to some people we'd be halfway west across the mountains looking for a new home, halfway across the island.'

'And leaving our crops,' Johnny Rain Bird nodded.

Nanny shook her head. 'We should name this town for all of us who never make it this far. All of us who dead and gone, or still working our hearts and hands sore for massa all across the island.'

Everyone went quiet. Everyone knew someone somewhere else.

Hester broke the silence. 'So we use your name, Nanny. To stand for all of them, all of us. Those gone and those to come.'

There was a murmur of agreement.

Nanny went to speak again. Everyone was looking at her, but Johnny Rain Bird put his hand up.

'Exactly. And you are the one to hold us together. To make certain we ready.'

Hester stood up. 'Is agreed,' she said. 'Take it as our thanks if you can't take it any other way. Honestly, Nanny, it an honour. It's deserved and there's no more to it.'

Nanny looked at her fellow villagers and nodded. It was a gift and she could not turn it down.

Something made Michele squeal, and she wriggled away. Quao's head hit the ground and he woke up suddenly.

'What is agreed? What?' he said, picking up his hat and putting it back on his head.

'This place,' Hester said. 'Here. It called Nanny Town now.'

The look on Quao's face was enough to make the whole village laugh.

But Nanny stood up, raised her hand to stop the laughter. 'We move together from now on. As one people. And we need to be united. Not against each other, arguing with each other. We may have won one battle but we have a war coming. Those Englishmen. They will not be content when they find out what happened here. It's not a matter of *if* they come, but *when*.'

The villagers shifted. Everyone knew she was right.

'We must make sure we always ready. We keep the tracks up to town covered. Make sure there is only one path into town from here. We make ambush, so that whenever one of those soldiers set foot in our forest they good as dead. We have to look out for each other to stay free. We all one family now.'

Hester stood up. She began singing a song from the other side of the ocean. Some of the older folk knew the words, but the ones born on the island mumbled along and joined in as best they could. Nanny remembered it; it was about clear skies, and true friendship, and how families fought for each other. The whole village sang, and the melody seemed to soar up and above the trees, and Nanny would not have been surprised if the sound carried all the way back across the ocean and to their families far away.

Then Nanny thought that even though the home they were singing about was on the far side of an endless sea, that this place, this island, this bush, this forest was more of a home than anything else. That she and her new family would stay here for ever, free always, whatever it took, whether it was stories, or whether it was blood.

It was several moons after the battle. It almost seemed like a story now, Nanny thought; something that had happened to other people. Except for the times at night, just before she fell to sleeping, when she remembered the death of Shettlewood. At her own hand, face to face. That was the first time she had killed a man, close quarters, and even though she reminded herself that the world was a better place without him, it sometimes shook her awake. And she wondered how many more men she would have to kill with her own hands before the people she loved were free.

Nanny Town had grown. Nanny organized traps and ambushes for any soldiers who made it up the trails: massive boulders held in place with vines that could be cut, so they would rain down on their enemies. They covered wide trails and made sure the narrow ones had useful ambush points, so patrols could be picked off before they got too close.

And the town seemed to get bigger with every passing new moon. Quao led raids for cattle and supplies. And with every raid, still more people came to join them, to find freedom.

It wasn't all runaways that made Nanny Town grow. There were new babies – a little girl, named Clash after the battle, and two boys, Quarshie and Hopeful. The corn was ripening, sorrel and callaloo sprouted up faster than they could eat it, and the trees around dropped fruit.

But Nanny could see there was a problem. The cows weren't milking. One had sickened and died, too ill to eat, and the chickens were killed by some animal or other that came out of the bush one night and left a mess of feathers.

Then Quao told her there was another problem.

Nanny was chopping wood outside her cabin when he came by.

'I need to talk with you, Miss Nanny.'

'Miss, is it now?' Nanny put down her axe. 'This must be bad news.'

'We have to do something,' he said, lighting up a tobacco pipe. 'This about guns. The little raids use ammunition, faster than we getting it. We need a bigger raid, we need more musket, more rifle. More cutlass.'

Nanny went to speak, but Quao stopped her.
'I know we can pick off the patrols, the threes and fours of redcoats that come looking. The slaves they have working for them, those men they call the Black Shot…'

'The Black Shot? They like trees without roots. I hear they have nothing to lose and the Englishmen take out their souls.' Nanny kissed her teeth. 'Have they forgotten who is the enemy here?'

Quao nodded. 'Those men will do anything. Kill us soon as look at us. They won't be so easily tricked into ambush… I hear they kill a party of children in Cudjoe's town one time.'

'I see it, Quao,' Nanny said. 'I know another big battle come soon enough.'

Quao nodded. 'When the redcoats come back, in force, we be just like them chickens, spread out dead and featherless.'

Nanny sat down, and motioned Quao to sit too.

'I think we make a big raid,' he said. 'And I have an idea.' He sat down. 'I know in the past I been wrong-headed, about you, about this place.' He looked round the village. Nanny looked too. Some children were playing with Michele, dressing her in a bonnet made of leaves. Hester Jane sat outside her cabin sewing. It was peaceful, it was home. 'I'm not thinking to join with Cudjoe right now. I'm staying put.'

Nanny nodded. 'You are right this time, Quao. We have to do something. Johnny Rain Bird tell me the corn might fail. We need to show the English that whatever they send against us they cannot win. They need to know we are a force they cannot move,' she said. 'Then maybe they leave us alone.'

Quao put out his hand. 'We agreed.' He paused. 'Also...' He took his three-cornered hat off and ran the brim through his hands. 'I have some business I need to finish. I been thinking, Nanny. We go to Mount Vernon, they have plenty guns. They have enough food. We go in when the moon is waning and the sky dark. It three days there and three days back.'

'Mount Vernon? The place you run from in St George? I thought you terrified?'

'Maybe,' Quao nodded. 'But I know the lie of the land. And like I said, Nanny Town needs the guns.' He puffed on his pipe and the smoke curled up into the air.

Nanny thought for a long moment. She looked at him, remembered how scared he'd been of the overseer, Mr Michael Noach. Saw how much he wanted to help the town grow now. She nodded. 'A small raiding party, but we make a big show. We can't afford to lose anyone…'

'Agreed. I thought Johnny Rain Bird and Nestor, one of the new fellows.'

Nanny shook her head. 'Not him. If anyone taking risks for Nanny Town it have to be me.' She smiled. 'And maybe you were right about Obeah. The gods can help us whip their guns and supplies from under their noses.'

'I thought you did not believe, Nanny?'

Nanny shrugged. 'I coming round, Quao…'

Quao smiled.

Ophelia came to Nanny Town the day before they set off, leading her white mule Treasure, out of the bush track and into the open space where there were meetings and dancing. Ophelia burned some bush herbs Nanny didn't know the name of and made her and Quao and Johnny Rain Bird breathe in the smoke.

'It for protection,' Ophelia said. 'You have the herbs inside you, then bullets fly from you like rain down a mountainside.'

Nanny didn't argue. The smell was bitter and caught on the back of her throat. She thought about the tales she had heard when she was young, long ago on the other side of that massive sea. Weren't there people who could catch bullets? In their hands? She looked down through the smoke at her own weather-beaten palms. They had survived so much. Surely they could survive anything.

Then Ophelia took her right hand and looked at it. 'This the hand that take a life,' she said, tracing the lines and furrows. 'It have to kill again,' Ophelia said, and Nanny swallowed. 'In the meantime, take this.' Ophelia folded something small and metal into her palm. Nanny couldn't see it, but she knew it was a bullet from the cold metal and the shape.

'You remember, your hand enfold it, close on it.' Nanny's eyes grew wide. Had Ophelia been listening to her thoughts? Had she told the tale about catching bullets out loud?

Ophelia leaned close and whispered the words into her ear so only she could hear. 'Town depend on you. You remember you can do anything, Nanny. Nothing stronger than you, nothing fiercer than you. Not on this whole island. Maybe not in the world.'

It was a week later they set out west through the bush. Nanny walked the road, cutlass hidden in the folds of her skirts, Yaw's knife in her belt, leading Ophelia's mule that she'd lent them for the journey. The baskets on the mule's back were empty now, but she'd be useful on the way home. Quao and Johnny Rain Bird kept to the bush. At night they made camp and slept under the trees, the moon winking at them through the leaf canopy, the frogs and the night birds singing them to sleep.

Nanny felt the fear building as they came closer.

On the third day they reached Mount Vernon. It was the biggest plantation Nanny had ever seen. Quao led them around the edge of the estate, past the acres of cane – taller than a man with leaves so sharp they could tear skin – that surrounded the house like a rolling green sea. Before they saw anything they heard the sound of the work gangs, and saw the overseers on their horses, whips in hand.

Then, almost as big as Nanny Town, there was the village of slave huts and tiny gardens. The plantation house stood by itself, white and shining, with the smaller overseers' cottages close by. Then, on the edge of the estate, there was a sugar mill, driven by horses, to crush the ripe cane, and the refineries where the slaves worked day and night to boil the sugar in giant copper pans.

'There are so many people,' Johnny Rain Bird said, and Nanny could hear his fear. 'How we get anything out of there?'

Nanny swallowed. She was thinking the exact same thing. They wouldn't have the advantage of putting fear into the hearts of their enemies here.

'The guns in store near the house,' Quao said.
'I know where the keys are. It's possible. We need a
distraction, though, and I'm thinking you and Nanny
set one over the refinery, get as many buckra out of
the house and away while I'm working.'

Johnny Rain Bird whistled. 'We going to need
all the luck.' Nanny saw he put his hand up to the
charms around his neck.

Nanny looked down at the slaves, bent double
carrying loads of cane into the crushing teeth of the
mill. She thought they would need more than luck:
they would need help. She looked closer. One of the
mounted overseers cracked his whip in the air.

Johnny saw her watching. 'That man, on the
horse?' he said. The overseer hit out again, and a
slave – tall, strong, but bent double with cane –
stumbled, his load of sugar cane rolling off his back.

Quao pointed. 'That one the overseer, name of
Noach. Him a demon in human skin. If there was a
way to kill him dead tonight, I will do it.'

Nanny realized she wasn't looking at the overseer.
She had recognized the tall slave Noach had hit. He
was the man from the slave auction in Albany. It was
him! And as he got up and gathered his load again she
could see his anger burned so strong she could feel it
from their hiding place. What was his name? Adou.
That was it. Adou.

'I think,' Nanny said, 'I might have an idea myself.'

6

CATCHING BULLETS

Mount Vernon Estate

Night fell hard and fast. There was no moon and the darkness came down like a heavy curtain.

Quao did not think much of Nanny's idea. 'These people broken!' he said. 'If they step out of line, the skin flay off their back, or worse their children's backs! We can't ask them to help.'

Nanny stood firm. 'They the same as us! We give them a chance. And I know some of them so soon off the boat they have nothing to lose.'

'They raise the alarm we all dead,' Johnny Rain Bird said.

'We all dead' – Nanny brushed down her skirt.

She felt Yaw's knife there and it made her feel strong – 'sooner or later.' She didn't wait to hear any more argument. 'I'm taking the tinderbox. When you see the flames and hear the alarm you fetch as much grain and rifles as you can carry. Leave me to burn the mill down to the ground.'

Nanny walked away without turning back. She headed out of the trees towards the slave village.

In the centre of the village she could see some cooking fires lit and Nanny kept her head up. A chicken almost ran past her followed by a small child. Nanny stopped him. 'You know Adou?' she asked; her heart was thumping but she kept her voice smooth and soft.

The child looked up at her. In the dark his eyes shone. 'Him live at the end there,' the child said, 'but him name Caesar now.'

Nanny could still remember her mother's language from the other side of the ocean. She knew it when she heard it, not just the sound of each word, but the sense of meaning in the rising and falling, the music it made. So she took herself to the huts farthest away from the fires and listened. She could hear one man wincing in pain as another spoke – was that Coromantee? Was he being told to stay still? Even though she couldn't make out all the words, she would bet it was. Nanny took a deep breath. For strength, she felt the cutlass in her skirt and the charms around her neck.

'Adou!' She said it like a loud whisper, and the voices fell silent. 'Adou!' she called again.

Then she stepped out from behind the hut and looked at him. It was the same man, she was certain.

'Adou!' Nanny said. He had a bowlful of water and some aloe leaves — she could smell them — and he was bathing another man's back. Even in the weak firelight she could see that the man's back was glistening, sore. She spoke in a rush. 'I am Nanny. I am from the free town of the Maroons. We need your help.'

He said nothing for a long moment. Somewhere a child cried and a woman was arguing with a man in a hut a little way off.

It seemed to Nanny that his silence went on for ever.

She stepped away from the hut back into the darkness. 'I am setting fires,' she said. 'We come to burn the sugar mill down tonight. You could be free. With us.'

'You have a spark?'

'I have a tinderbox,' Nanny replied.

'*Medaase!*' he said, and dropping the bowl of water, fell to the ground in front of her. 'Thanks to you! We have been praying to see a way out and now you are here.'

Nanny stepped back. 'This will not be easy. I cannot promise—'

'We know.' Adou got up. 'We know what these people are. We will go with you. There will be others.' He looked at her. 'You have guns?' he said.

Nanny shook her head. For a moment she thought he would change his mind, refuse to come. His brow was high and his eyes shone. He took her hand the way Ophelia had. 'You have something else. You have Obeah. I feel it.'

Nanny did not know what to say. She felt the same woman as she ever was. But there was a kind of fizzy power in her touch. The same power she had felt that day by the waterfall. She looked back at him. 'Come, then,' she said at last. 'All of you.' Then she set off towards the refinery.

The man with the flayed back followed too. 'This is Kofi.' Adou hurried to catch up. 'He is like my brother.'

Nanny nodded. 'Good. It's good.' She put her hand up to the charms around her neck. She felt the shape of the bullet in there in among the twigs and bones.

'This way quicker,' Adou said, and took her hand, and Nanny felt suddenly as if the old gods were walking with her as he led her through the darkness and into the trees.

When they came out of the trees and into the edge of the clearing they could see the fires in the sugar refinery were still burning.

'It's harvest now,' Adou said. 'No stopping. Buckra have us working and working. One day, then the next is night.'

Kofi nodded. 'I slump down, I was asleep standing up. That's why buckra flay me so.'

Nanny could see the roof was made of thatch. 'Can we set the roof of the mill alight?'

Adou nodded. 'I show you.'

He and Kofi collected dry leaves and twigs, then bound them into makeshift torches.

'We throw these on the mill roof,' he said.

'What about the refinery?' Nanny asked. 'We need them all to go up at the same time. We need to make sure those working are out.'

Adou nodded. 'We will spread the word. There is a song. If we start it the song will spread, and then the fire.'

Nanny took out the tinderbox. She coaxed the flames into life, and they lit the bundles and walked towards the buildings. Adou and Kofi began to sing. Their voices were low and strong, and soon Nanny heard it taken up by the slaves inside the boiling house, and then from further away, back in the slave village.

Before they had reached the refinery there came a shout from inside, and through the huge windows Nanny realized one of the coppers of boiling sugar had been turned over. Bubbling, burning sugar was snaking out across the floor.

Nanny watched Adou crouching low to lob his flaming leaves inside, and the sugar caught instantly, the fire shooting up into a sheet of flame.

Then she remembered she had a job to do too, and she made her way to the quiet mill and threw her torch up onto the roof. For a moment nothing happened. All around her it seemed as if the night had come to life. There were shouts of *Fire!* and the crack and snap of burning from the refinery, people running, yelling – but the mill was still quiet and dark.

Then she was certain she heard the sound of hooves coming from the big house, and just as one of the overseers rounded the track from the house, shirt flapping, his pale horse wild, the roof blossomed into yellow orange red flames.

Would this be enough for Quao and Johnny Rain Bird?

In moments there were people everywhere. The boiling-house slaves were running out into the night. A white man in a white shirt was shouting and the fleeing slaves scattered.

Nanny saw the man on horseback thunder towards them. She saw the man – and was it Noach, the man Quao said was a devil? – take the handgun from his belt, and fire towards where Adou and Kofi were helping people to safety, out of the blazing refinery.

Hadn't Quao said this place was full of demons? It seemed, thought Nanny, as if the mouth of hell open up wide, and maybe all of them could be swallowed right up.

Without thinking she stood up, stepped out of the dark into the moving orange firelight. When she thought about it afterwards she realized she could remember every single detail, as if she was running slow when the world around her was running fast. There was a crack-crack-crack as the buckra fired his gun.

She told Ophelia afterwards it was as if she felt like a tree: her feet were on the ground, but it was like there were roots, lines of power going deep down and running up through her. Power from a thousand thousand spirits of all the people that had come before her and might perhaps come afterwards. It was in that fizzing she'd felt from Adou's touch that burned inside her. And there was that smell of the herbs, catching in her throat.

Nanny put out a hand. She could feel the air change as the bullets flew towards her, cutting through the air like tiny, lethal, metal knives.

She knew if she did nothing someone would die. She put her hand up. Something happened. A sharp sting, but no more than that. Had she caught that bullet in her hand? She felt as strong as a mountain. She put her hand out again and closed it around heat and air and death.

'Run!' she shouted to the others as loud as she could. 'Into the trees!'

The pale horse reared up, snorting, its iron shoes catching the light. The man stayed on and wheeled around. She felt him looking straight at her. He put his gun up to his sightline. He fired again.

Nanny did not move. She knew now he could not kill her while she felt like this. And something told her that if, by a kind of miracle, he did, it would not matter. He was dead inside, this man. He was, as Quao had said, a kind of devil in human skin.

He shot again. Three hard sharp cracks.

Nanny breathed in and stood firm. In that instant she was absolutely certain that she was fiercer than anyone, and she was stronger than anyone.

'You see,' Quao was leading the white mule, now loaded up with rifles and sacks of grain and salt fish. He was talking to Adou who walked alongside, hefting yet another full sack of flour. He was in full flow, recounting the tale he had told at least three times since they'd left Mount Vernon.

Quao went on, 'I find the buckra name of Noach, pull him down off his mighty horse and I slit his throat. Neck to gullet! So!' He mimed a cutting motion. 'Then I take the key off him and steal every one of their rifle.' Quao cast a look towards a young woman in a faded blue headwrap, and she smiled back at him.

Johnny Rain Bird laughed. 'Way you tell it, you think it you and you alone!'

Quao made a face.

There were nine of them walking along the bush trail, high up in the mountains and as far away from the road as possible. Six of them were Mount Vernon people taking their chance to escape out of the chaos: Adou and Kofi, Katy in the blue headwrap, Phoebe and her light-skin baby Thomboy, tucked into her shawl, and a man as big as a house, name of Atlas, whose nose had been split – he said this was the fourth time he had run from Mount Vernon.

'I never thought I get the chance again,' he said, and Nanny saw there were a few tears running down his face.

'I never believe what happen,' Kofi said, 'if I didn't see it myself.'

Johnny Rain Bird nodded. 'See Nanny? She pluck those bullets clean out of the air!'

'Oh, I don't know…' Nanny put a hand up to the gris gris around her neck. In the tiny cloth bag there were six bullets now.

'You too modest, Miss Nanny,' Adou said.

Quao kissed his teeth.

'I'm not certain what happen,' Nanny said. 'I put myself in the lap of the spirits.'

'You have Obeah. It's strong in you,' Adou said.

'I think it must be.' Nanny smiled.

'No wonder then the whole town name after you,' Adou said, and smiled back.

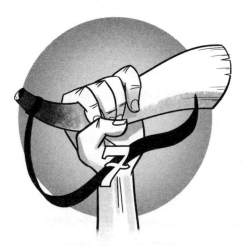

A CLOUD OF TROUBLES

Nanny Town, Blue Mountains

Six months later the crops were growing, they had some goats and the flock was larger month by month. The chickens they'd got from Mount Vernon were excellent layers. And since that raid, new folk had made their way to freedom from plantations as far south as Morant Bay and as far west as Spanish Town. They grew plantain and mountain cabbage, yams and peas and pumpkin. And there were at least two hundred people living free in Nanny Town now.

Ophelia brought news that the redcoats were terrified, that Nanny's legend had grown: she was an Obeah woman who could conjure whirlpools and catch bullets in her hands. There was even talk she could kill a man with one look!

Patrols into the bush dwindled. Malaria and yellow fever killed so many English soldiers and seemed to have weakened the others. Ophelia said the camp at Bagnall's Thicket resembled nothing more than an outdoor hospital where men sickened and died in their hundreds. She and Nanny sat in the shade shelling gungo peas and looking out at the village.

'They bring in more Black Shot fighters,' Ophelia said. 'Slave folk to fight their battles.'

'The Black Shot?' Nanny shook her head. 'We seen them! They join up to get away from cutting cane and fieldwork.' Nanny waved a hand. 'They youths who want to hold a gun, and think it make them free. I thought they would be hard, but they are all like eggs, boys with shells of fierceness hiding soft soft innards.' Nanny tipped some peas into her basket. 'I taught the children here to trick them, stand at the end of the gully and wave then hide. The Black Shot run into our ambush like rabbits into holes.' Nanny shrugged. 'Most of them, well, it a shame to kill them. Some run into the bush and we find them a few days later. Some choose to stay with us. Choose freedom.' Nanny sat back. 'The garden need work right now, Ophelia,' Nanny said. 'We are protected up here. Safe.'

'For now. The English are not about to give up this island,' Ophelia said. 'They go come after you, only a matter of time. Remember that.'

As Ophelia was leaving, Nanny found her a cloth bag full of pumpkin seeds. 'Take these, harvest good this season.'

Ophelia smiled and folded the bag back into Nanny's hand. 'You keep them. You never know when they needed…'

Ophelia went home before dark and Nanny went back to work in her garden. She had begun to clear a new patch of ground, but there was a massive old tree root that needed pulling up. She had dug around it, tried levering it up, but it would not budge. She'd chopped as much of it out as she could but the root and the bottom of the trunk stubbornly refused to budge. Nanny paused for a moment, taking a breath, resting on her axe.

'Miss Nanny!' Adou called out. 'You need some help with that?'

Nanny waved him across. 'Come on, it will be easy with two.'

Afterwards, Nanny made some ginger tea and Adou talked about home.

'I had a woman, name of Ama,' he said, 'and a baby. And cattle. Had a good number head of cattle.' He looked into the distance, and Nanny could feel the weight of sadness coming from him.

'My family die on the ship. I saw their bodies go into the water.'

Nanny said nothing.

'Why they do this to us, you think?' he said.

Nanny looked at him. 'Because they can.'

'What happen to you?' he said, looking at Nanny. 'How did you get here?'

Nanny looked away over the town and into the trees. 'I never think about my life before now, before here.' She shrugged. 'I can't think about them take me anywhere, so I tell myself there was nothing before Nanny Town. I was never a girl running alongside my mother to market. I was never taken, held down until they tie my hand and foot to get me on a boat, sell my children from me. I was never whipped. I was never a slave.'

She smiled a strong, fierce smile.

'I believe I always been free. In my heart.'

Hurricane season was late, but Nanny had made sure the town had enough supplies and cattle to get through it. Hester and Phoebe traded some cloth for baskets, and there was an ease to town life Nanny had never felt before. She watched some of the boys practising dances in the town square with Atlas, and Meggy chasing Michele the pig out of the bush and laughing and laughing. Nanny smiled. She had never felt more safe in her whole life.

Then one night, another joyful night when one of Johnny's cows gave birth to a female calf – a good sign, if one was needed – and Phoebe's little boy had started walking, Nanny dreamed about Yaw.

In her dream he came towards her, standing upright, ruined, face sad, calling for his pig, Michele. In the dream Nanny took his hand, holding it between both of hers and not being able to look too long at his shot-up face, the blood, the bone. She asked him though, in as still and calm a voice as she could manage, 'What do you want with us, Yaw? Why aren't you quiet, safe across the water, home? The British drop like flies, malaria wipe them out before long. You seen us in town, even Michele your pig happy.'

His answer came fast and loud. 'Nuh-uh.' He shook his head. 'Something is happening. Maybe this time even you cannot stop it, Nanny.'

The boy turned back to the bush and Nanny thought that there was something moving, there in the corner of her eye. Yaw was pointing through the trees. A man, small if it was a man, golden-skinned. Running, flashing through the green.

'There,' Yaw said and Nanny woke as if a bucket of water had been thrown over her, sitting bolt upright, her heart galloping fast fast time.

Outside it was not yet light, everything was grey and colourless. The whole town still slept.

Nanny stumbled out of her hut and went to her garden and wept. They would never be safe.

In the morning she walked out of town and visited Ophelia. The woman saw her coming as she was outside working in the garden.

'I see you walking out of the trees with a cloud of troubles following you.' Ophelia put down her pruning knife. She took Nanny to sit on the verandah and she held her hand and looked at the lines on her hand.

Nanny told her the dream. 'It shake me up.'

'You correct to be worried,' Ophelia said. 'See this line, here? There a break in it I never seen before. And something happen in Port Antonio, some new soldiers. New fighters. From overseas.'

Nanny nodded. 'It's been too easy.'

'The English angry as stinging ants,' Ophelia said. 'They new Governor, he bad man for you.'

'Governor? Don't they all do what their king say?' Nanny said.

'King George, yes. But he is over the water. The Governor is the King's man here. This new one, this Governor Gregory, he wants to change the way things are going. And change never any good for no one.'

'How? How so?'

'This governor fed up with you Maroons. The talk is he think you and Cudjoe mock the English…'

Nanny kissed her teeth. 'We don't mock anyone, we just want to be left alone.'

'They don't see that. They see your people, their property. They think they own all of us. They hate any of us to be free. We all know that is true.'

Nanny shifted in her seat.

Ophelia went on, 'English folk bursting with anger, so many slaves escape, throw off their masters and head into the bush. Others rise up and kill their masters. They scared. All the white people scared. This new governor promise them to make life safe for them to make money and to sleep in their beds. I think he means to stop the Maroons once and for all. Wipe you out.'

Nanny nodded. 'That's why Yaw come to me.' She took the herbs Ophelia offered, to make protecting tea and to guard against danger.

'You want me to look ahead? See what might happen?' Ophelia asked. 'It might help?'

Nanny shook her head. 'If the future bad, I'm not sure I want to know,' she said. 'I already feel in my bones, the fighting time come round again. Soon, soon.'

Ophelia nodded. 'You a different woman now. There is power in you.'

Nanny shook her head. 'Ophelia, I—'

'I know you feel the power of our ancestors in you. These hands – they catch bullets, I hear.'

'I don't know. I can't tell what happen, what really happen,' Nanny said. 'That just a tale…'

Ophelia looked hard at Nanny. 'You learn nothing yet? You *take* the story and make it *real*. Take that power, take the spirits of all of us, take whatever they say about you and make it your own. Then you can do whatever you need to for you, for your people.'

Nanny headed back to town and found Adou on the trail outside town waiting for her.

'I worried about you,' he said. 'You take all the worries of all of us on your shoulders, Nanny.'

Nanny shrugged. 'Town have my name, it's not a choice.'

'You pass some of that worry on to me. Let me help with that.'

She took his hand. Remembered the power she had felt the night of the raid at Mount Vernon.

'Adou,' Nanny said, 'I need you to help me with something else. We need to go to Port Antonio.'

The next morning she called a meeting and told the town what she and Adou would do. She would walk as far as Port Antonio, the largest town on the north coast, where the tall-masted ships came in, and find out exactly what the English were up to.

Hester and Johnny Rain Bird thought she was mad. 'We safe now!' Johnny said. 'It a waste of time! Little by little – and the day soon come – we

Maroons, we free people, will outnumber slaves. The English will sicken and die or flee to America and leave us alone.'

'He's right,' Kofi said. He was holding Phoebe's wriggling baby, Thom, in his arms and he put him down to walk away on his sturdy little legs. 'We safe here. It's been months since any soldiers even leave camp, let alone come up into the bush!'

Nanny smiled. 'I wish that were so. But I have to do something. Remember Yaw? He come to me in a dream. I cannot ignore him. And I cannot ignore what Ophelia say about new soldiers come, about the English plans.'

There was a murmur of agreement from the townspeople.

'So we will go. I take Adou. Quao, you are in charge while I am gone. Start preparing – I was thinking, we need to make more traps around town. Change the trails, make a retreat on Carrion Crow Mountain in case they find us here.'

Hester frowned. Johnny Rain Bird spoke up, 'Are you certain about this, Nanny...? Only we have work to do in the field and roofs need fixing up before the hurricanes—'

Quao interrupted. He nodded at Nanny. 'We start work on new traps.'

'It settled,' she said. 'I have to see with my own eyes whatever it is the British plan.' Nanny looked round as little Thom toppled over onto the ground and began to cry. Hester Jane picked him up. 'We have to keep Nanny Town, to keep all of us safe.'

BLACK SHOT AND MESKITO

Port Antonio

Nanny and Adou crested the road above the town and looked down on a beautiful scene. The sea sparkled, a shining bright blue like the tail of a hummingbird, and the green of the island trees seemed brighter and stronger than usual. Nanny felt her heart high and light, even with the thought they might find out if the rumours the English were up to something were true.

Hadn't they beaten them already? Weren't the redcoats terrified of disease and sickness, let alone that if they set foot in the bush Nanny's Obeah would swallow their spirits and kill them dead?

Nanny smiled. She looked across at Adou walking

along beside her and thought there wasn't anything she and her people couldn't do.

'Adou?' she said as they walked in step along the road. 'I was thinking, perhaps… perhaps I clear some land up by the east track out of town. Make a bigger garden.'

Adou smiled. 'I could help you with that,' he said, 'if you like. I can put in some cassava, and some corn, some pea…'

'I think that sound like a very good idea,' Nanny said, and they walked down the hill into Port Antonio together.

This morning, surely, Nanny thought, there were less white people on the street. Definitely fewer red-coated soldiers. The rum shops were quiet, only sailors waiting for the tide. Nanny felt herself relax and her heart lighten a little more. How could the English fight and win with less men?

She and Adou made a circuit of town and met at the market. They would buy provisions and trade some of Nanny Town's plantain and yam for cloth and twine, pots and pans.

The market was busy, stallholders setting out their wares on rush mats or banana leaves. Nanny passed men selling sacks of allspice, coffee berries, cocoa pods, ugly but delicious custard apple, pale orange mango and bright green guinep. There were some children singing for pennies, and a monkey that did tricks and a parrot that talked if you gave it an almond.

Nanny left Adou to fetch some flour while she walked around. Perhaps there would be gossip, some redcoats spending the day drinking rum, letting plans slip.

Then a shout made her look through the crowd. She followed the sound and found an old woman sitting by a small pyramid of ripe mangoes, all colours from green to bright red. She was being jeered at by six or seven rough-looking men. They were dressed like slaves, only each with a powder horn and musket slung about their chest. Their shoulders looked broad enough to knock down doors, and they picked up the stallholder's precious fruit and dashed it to the ground.

'You never pay me!' The old woman was desperate.

'Your fruit not worth a penny,' the broadest man said. He looked to be the oldest too, and he wore a battered redcoat's hat. 'We pay nothing for nothing.'

Nanny pushed her way closer. Some wore what looked like army jackets, only dark blue or black. Others were bare-chested. All carried a musket and cutlass.

These men, these men who looked like slaves, had weapons. Nanny did not stop to think; she stood herself between the men and the stallholder.

'You have no respect!' she said, drawing herself up and glaring.

The men laughed. 'Who you to tell us anything? We don't take orders from no woman.' The army hat man leaned close. His breath stank of rum and Nanny could see the brand on his chest, but she didn't recognize it. His owner not from round here? Or was he one of Cudjoe's men strayed east? They would not be so rude, surely?

One of the men picked up a mango and took a bite, then kicked over the remaining fruit. The old woman wailed.

'Eh! You! Rusticutters!' Nanny said. 'You pay for that!'

Army hat man spat on the ground in front of her. 'This none of your business. My men do as they please. Take it up with our master.' The rest of the men surrounded them, just like a pack of dogs, Nanny thought. She stood firm – she knew never to be afraid of dogs.

They were definitely Black Shot. She had faced worse than this a thousand times.

'I am not afraid. Not of you, or your masters. I am not afraid of anyone.'

The men laughed. Three-cornered hat man glanced down at the charms around her neck.

'Well you should be,' the man said. 'We are the Black Shot, and we here to hunt.'

Nanny wanted to laugh. She looked around at the men. Their leader was steadfast but she could see some of the others were wavering. They were not much more than youths.

'You heard of Obeah?' she said, her voice steady and low. 'You heard of the spirits and duppy that live up in those hills?' She jutted her chin towards the mountains to the south. 'I hear there a woman up there can catch bullets in her hand...'

'We heard of the witch!' one of them said. 'Name of Nanny! I hear she have fangs and walk upon hooves.'

'She a hag!'

Nanny kept her face steady even though she wanted to smile. 'Uh-huh, I hear that too. I would be mightily scared if I were you.'

'Witches?' another said. 'Do we look like children?'

Nanny resisted answering 'Yes'.

'We will find her,' one of the men said, his tone braver. 'We will take her apart limb by limb.'

Nanny stepped closer, spoke low. 'Not if she put spell on you first. She killed armies of English men, she kill you too. She shrivel you up, simple as that.' Nanny snapped her fingers. 'You see ant on your foot? You wake up in the night screaming as those red biting ants cover you up like a wave of water and leave nothing but shining bone.'

The man in the hat laughed as he led his men away, but Nanny could see some of the others were shaken.

Only the leader turned round to glare at her, but Nanny sent a look so strong and so sharp she was certain it would cut him down. And she knew the memory of that look would wound – perhaps, as he tried to sleep that evening, he would not be able to close his eyes.

The stallholder was still sobbing. Nanny helped her recover the fruit that was undamaged and let her have some of the guinep she had brought from home to sell.

'Tell me, mother,' Nanny asked, as she helped arrange the mangoes. 'How many of them loutish Black Shot you seen around town?'

The old woman dabbed at her eyes with her skirts. 'Huh! Them lout indeed.'

'True, true. You have numbers, a dozen dozen perhaps? More?'

The old woman made a face, thinking. 'There are many of them, enough to fill up a half this marketplace, I reckon. They make a little camp out away from town, come from Leeward so. Saint Elizabeth and Hanover. I think they fight the Maroons.' The old woman leaned close. 'Me tell you something, daughter. I hope the Maroons sweep the lot of them Black Shot into the sea!'

The old woman laughed. And as Nanny walked away she felt taller, stronger. There would be fights, but they would win.

Adou was coming towards her through the crowd, his face set hard. She waved. He came over, took her by the arm and led her away from the marketplace and towards the dockside. 'You must see this,' he said.

A flock of small boats – fishing boats, row boats – were clustered at the quay, while just out in the bay the massive three- and four-masted sailing ships waited at anchor. The ships looked like huge wooden towns. For a second Nanny thought she remembered the sound and the smell and she felt sick just imagining setting foot again on one of those things.

'Look!' Adou pointed further up the quayside.

Nanny looked away from the ships and followed his gaze. There were men unloading from ten, twenty small boats. Not English redcoats, not Black Shot youths, but men: wiry, lean-muscled men with straight black hair and golden skin. Some only wore breeches, some wore a cloth around their hips; some had boots, some did not.

Watching, Nanny felt a kind of cold dread. Had they been in the dream with Yaw? Just out of sight? Those golden men?

'Who are they?' Nanny asked.

'Those people called Meskito. They from the mainland, the Gulf of Honduras, land called Belize. I ask a sailor. He tell me they come to kill Maroons. They never sicken, they never die and they have their own spirits. From what I gather from talking to some of the sailors, they have no fear of ours.'

Nanny watched. And for a moment her heart sank.

She was quiet on the walk home.

Adou took her hand in his and told her what else he had learned. That the English were building a new camp and widening the roads up into the mountains. That more redcoats and Black Shot and Meskito were coming. That heavy guns were going to be moved from Bagnall's Thicket. And that there were dogs to track them through the bush. Packs of dogs.

They walked home a different way, over to the east towards where the building work Adou described had begun. There was a massive scar in the forest, with broken trees torn up or sawn down, and gangs of men clearing bush and scrub. The road, just as Adou said, pushed up into the bush and was easily, Nanny reckoned, wide enough for six men to march side by side across it. Nanny could see them in her mind's eye: too many to pick off one by one, and maybe hauling those big guns that fired cannonballs. Could they flatten out a road all the way up to Nanny Town?

She was silent, listening, thinking as they passed. There were so many children in the town now, she had to keep them all safe. Every one. Her heart would break.

Once they reached the safety of the trail, Nanny spoke. 'We start work tomorrow,' she said. 'Set up more traps, hang more rocks above the trails. If they come for us we will make sure that they regret it. Obeah and stories is not enough. We must all be warriors now, every one of us, women and children too. They will not take our freedom from us again.'

When they reached home the stars were coming out, there was music somewhere and she could smell cooking, jerk pork, perhaps. It smelled so good. Nanny suddenly felt the weight of everyone's hopes and fears. She stopped and leaned against Adou a little. He did not move away.

Nanny shut her eyes and listened to her people, happy, unaware of the coming battle. She wished she knew of a way to stop time: to keep the world just as it was at that moment – the shouts of the children, the music. She would have given anything to stop the setting and rising of the sun, the moon changing. Nanny mumbled a prayer to the spirits of the ancestors and Adou whispered along with her.

Up in the tree canopy a bird called long and sharp and broke the spell. She and Adou set off on the last steps to Nanny Town.

'There one more thing, Adou.' She took his hand in hers. 'If you wanted, when the battle done, we could marry…'

There was a long moment, and Nanny remembered the time she had met him in Mount Vernon. How that silence had stretched on for ever.

She looked away. She should not ask, after all she had her people to think of, not just one man.

Then Adou squeezed her hand and spoke so gently it might have been music. 'Naturally,' he said, and she knew the power of the ancestors was in him too.

'*Medaase,*' Nanny said. '*Medaase*, Adou.' And then they walked into town together.

9

THE BATTLE FOR NANNY TOWN

The next evening Quao sat down with Nanny and Adou, after a long day tying rocks with vines ready to rain down on the soldiers' heads.

'Every day I send my thoughts down to where those English build their road,' Nanny said. 'In my mind I send them red ants and biting scorpion. And it not enough.'

Adou nodded. 'We were down there today,' he said. 'Every day the English eat up more of the trees, ploughing through the forest like an alligator snapping up the bush with heavy sharp jaws.' Adou built up the fire. 'That road will be broad and wide. We need hurricane to wash them away. I tell everyone I meet same same thing.'

'I see it this way,' Quao said. He took a stick and drew a plan of Nanny Town and the road, in the dirt by the fire. 'They closer every day. I reckon unless the hurricane come they attack when the moon full next. We need the whole town rise up…'

Adou nodded. 'Nanny, you say Obeah not enough. And you right. But it not only the redcoats and the Black Shot have to believe in them stories if we want to win. Nanny Town have to believe it too.'

Nanny looked up into the sky, following the sparks as they burned bright and vanished. That's what her life should be like, she thought, everyone's life, blazing and fierce, however long, however short it was.

Adou was right. If the whole town was going to fight, they were going to need to trust that they had magic on their side.

Nanny planned a ceremony as soon as possible. Adou and Quao put the word around, that she was going to call on the spirits to protect them. Nanny sent Meggy to visit Ophelia with a message to come back up to town, to help Nanny brew up a drink to turn the town of farmers back into warriors. To help Nanny find the words to make the story she needed.

Nanny waited for Ophelia on the track, hoping she would see her coming with her old white mule and her baskets full of herbs. But it was only Meggy, running, out of breath. Meggy doubled over a moment, hands on her knees. 'She sick, Miss Nanny.'

'Sick? Ophelia? How so? Should I go to her?' Nanny asked, worried.

Meggy straightened up, shook her head. 'No, Miss Nanny. She tell me to tell you it all right.' Meggy paused. 'In the end…' Meggy unwrapped a bundle of herbs and handed it over.

'How she look to you, Meggy? Miss Ophelia?'

Meggy shrugged. 'Like she need a good night's sleep…'

Nanny felt a tightness in her chest. Meggy ran ahead into town, her steps light and carefree, and Nanny wished she was a girl again. Then up ahead Meggy stopped and turned around.

'Oh! I nearly forget.' Meggy waited for Nanny to catch up. 'Miss Ophelia say to tell you one more thing.'

'She did?' Nanny thought there must be something, some charm, some spell of words to get her and her people through the coming battle. 'What was it, child?'

Meggy frowned, as if she was trying to remember. 'She say whatever you do, don't forget… forget some seeds or somesuch…' And Meggy ran off.

'Seeds? What seeds she mean?' Nanny shouted after her, but the girl had gone.

Quao brought word that the first troops had been sent west and Cudjoe's people were under sufferance: that they fought for their existence, and that dogs hunted them through the hills of the Cockpit Country where they lived. When the ceremony came, the town was eager to hear Nanny speak, eager to hear she could save them.

She was stirring a big pot as everyone gathered in the town square. Some of the children had helped fetch the herbs for the brew, but she had not told any of them what it was for. So rumours had been running all over town about the potion. Just as she wanted. She still wished Ophelia could have been here – but she knew the old woman would have approved. Now she saw the anticipation as she stirred, waiting for everyone to arrive and settle down.

'Ophelia tell me about this brew,' she said, which was mostly true. She'd had to improvise some of the ingredients. She had done a good job, though, she thought. The liquid in the pot was thick and dark and had a heady smell that made it seem powerful. 'We all know trouble coming. The English bringing soldiers and dogs. Black Shot and Meskito. I see them in my dreams, but I see them down the docks too.' There was a murmur of agreement and unease.

'We fight them before. And we win,' Nanny went on. Someone in the crowd cheered – Johnny Rain Bird. Nanny nodded to him. 'But this time we need more. This time, whole town must fight. That why I brew this potion. Everyone who drink it will feel the power of our ancestors. This potion strength and protection.'

There was whispering around her. Nanny couldn't tell if it was disbelief or excitement. She tried to ignore it, tried to think of how Ophelia sounded when she read her palm, to remember the feeling of power running through her as she swung her cutlass. 'We drink from this pot and we remember what we fighting for. For our home. For our family.' She met Adou's eye. 'For freedom!'

Adou lifted his hand and cheered. Nanny felt as if some of the heat of the fire was drawn into her, warm and strong. She lifted a cup.

'We have built Nanny Town together. Now we protect it.'

Since the ceremony, the mood in Nanny Town was more diligent, more determined. But Nanny found it harder to sleep. She felt the danger coming closer every day. She was doing all she could, but what if it was not enough?

Every day when she walked the path down to the river she expected to see those Meskito fighters slipping through the trees. Sometimes she thought she did, but it was just the sunlight moving through the shivering leaves.

What had happened with the bullets? Adou swore she had caught them. But however hard she tried to remember, the memory slipped away, as if it had been someone else there that night.

Everyone was busy, preparing for the coming attack. Children made piles of small stones ready to throw. Some adults sharpened cutlasses and knives, others left animal bones and monkey paws, signs of Obeah, nailed up to tree trunks or in the path.

But Nanny kept the thought of her wedding bright in her mind. Even as the moon grew fat and full and the battle drew nearer.

Quao had promised her and Adou a gift, and when he showed her the new carved handles he had made for her cutlasses and the fine milking cow, with her calf at foot, that he had raided from a plantation far to the east, Nanny hugged him. 'This cow,' she said. 'She belong to all of us.'

Nanny planned to give Adou the thing she held most precious: Yaw's knife, small and perfect. 'It save my life many times just by being there,' she told him. 'He is always with me, and soon you will be too.'

But the soldiers came when the moon was still full, in the hour before the sun came up. Nanny's people heard the dogs first; Quao came crashing into town to raise the alarm.

'They coming!' He was out of breath, the sweat shining on his chest. 'Three packs at least, barking to raise the dead.'

Nanny was up and had her cutlasses belted quick-sharp. The sound of the abeng soon echoed round camp and she sent Kwame to organize the younger children to the safety of Carrion Crow Mountain. If all failed, they would retreat there. The older ones she sent with Adou. He pulled her aside before he left, taking her hand in his. 'Nanny,' he said, his face close, for only her to hear. 'Do not worry. We will drive them away.'

His hand was warm. Nanny squeezed it tight. 'There so many of them. If we have to retreat...'

He shook his head. 'I see you up the hill then,' he told her. 'Even if we have to leave Nanny Town – come new moon, we be married. Remember.'

And then he was gone, leading the older children away to cut the vines and loose rocks.

Quao had led the most seasoned fighters down away from the town to try and cut off the soldiers' attack. But the dogs were still coming, and Nanny had just loaded her rifle when two of the Meskito fighters, skin oiled under their open jackets, came out of the forest in front of her. For a tiny moment Nanny froze. Then she remembered what Ophelia said, tried to remember the power she knew must still be in her, and put up her gun. At that instant behind her there was an almighty explosion. It was so loud and so hard that the ground under her feet shook.

Nanny felt her ears ringing. There was a light too, sudden and instant, bright orange-yellow. Then another explosion, and another. She staggered back. The Meskito were shouting – she could see their mouths moving, but the ringing in her ears made it so she could not hear them. She lifted her cutlass. Behind her the light was instantly brighter, and for a small moment she thought that dawn might have come early and all at once. Then she smelled it. The burning. She turned around, away from the men, and ran towards town as fast as she could.

Everything was on fire. The cannon had flattened Hester's hut and Johnny Rain Bird's too, and most of the others were burning. The animals ran through the wreckage, terrified.

Nanny felt a bullet whistle towards her. Without thinking she lifted her hand to catch it, but missed, and it grazed her skin, her bodice blooming a red flower of blood. Her heart pounded in her chest. The pain paled next to the sting of shame. Had it really all been imagined? Did she have no power at all?

Her ears still rang and rang. Her mouth and nose filled up with smoke as she ran. Everything felt unreal, and yet at the same time, the terrible feeling swelled inside her that everything until now had been some illusion, and it was only now that reality was rolling down on her. All around her, soldiers, Meskito and men of the Black Shot, dogs and redcoats burst out of the forest and into the centre of Nanny Town. They kicked over cooking pots and shot at the goats that had been bought for the wedding. They knifed the cow along her flank and lifted the calf away. And she could do nothing to stop them.

Through the drifting smoke she saw a shape run alongside her. It was Phoebe, but as Nanny reached for her hand Phoebe seemed to stop and crumble, fold to the ground.

'Phoebe!' Nanny cried, but she only heard it as a mumble.

She leaned down beside her, saw her eyes wide, frozen. Nanny felt for a pulse but there was none. She was about to get up when she saw something moving – it was Phoebe's little boy, Thom, underneath her, still alive, mouth open and wailing. Nanny could not hear a thing, only feel the vibration as she tore the boy from his mother and ran. As she did, she took the abeng that hung from her belt and sounded the alarm.

Michele the pig suddenly shot out of a hut and almost knocked Nanny off her feet. Nanny held tight to the baby and followed Michele out of the burning town, and found herself on the trail up to Carrion Crow Mountain.

Nanny coughed, and steadied herself. Michele was waiting on the path, looking round and almost wagging her small curly tail. Nanny gave thanks; perhaps the old gods had not quite deserted them.

She could feel Thom wriggling and crying, but for a tiny moment Nanny looked back at the town. There was only smoke and fire and destruction now. Her throat stung and her head felt thick and heavy. The pain in her shoulder burned. She turned away and started running again.

As she reached the lip of Carrion Crow Mountain she noticed a man on the ground. She thought first of all it was a heap of clothes – blue and white and brown and black and red. Shot to pieces. But it was what was left of a man…

Nanny stumbled and she almost lost her grip on Thom as Michele the pig snuffled over to the body. Because it *was* a body. Behind him were more dead – Efua, some of the children. Was that Meggy? She could not look. But the man, she realized, was Adou. Blasted apart, trying to protect the others.

Nanny stood alone on top of the mountain. Her hearing was just about coming back and she could hear shouts and barking and the crack-crack of gunfire.

She held tight to Thom and ran headlong into the bush. She felt the vine and leaf tear at the skin on her legs, pull at her clothes and the scarf around her hair. There were no tears as she went. She would not cry, even if it felt as if the forest had turned against them.

She ran faster. She cursed the English and the Meskito and the Black Shot and she hurtled down and down through the trees and towards the deepest gully in the mountains. And as Nanny ran the heavens opened. The wind roared and the rain came down in sheets.

As if the ancestors were crying the river of tears that she could not.

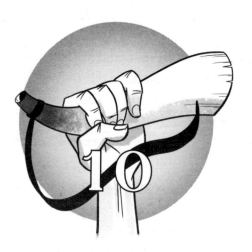

A NEW TRAIL

The rain saved them. The soldiers could not carry on; the new road, where the bush had been cleared, became a sea of mud. The rainfall was fierce and hard, each drop having the weight of a pebble or a stone, the wind fierce whipping the trees and blowing them all back down the mountain towards the sea.

There was so much rain it rushed and roared down the mountainsides and into the gullies like so many new rivers. Nanny and Thom sheltered inside a tree trunk with the frogs and lizards. The rain cascaded down between the leaves and down the vines, gathering strength and washing away their trail so the dogs and the Meskito fighters and the Black Shot could not track them.

Nanny did not sleep, could not sleep, but she held Thom while he did, and she felt the comfort of the island and the Obeah in every drop of water that thundered down onto the leaves with the force of gunshot. She hoped that Adou and Phoebe and Efua and the others would find their spirits flying back east across the ocean to where their ancestors would be waiting for them.

Before dawn she lay Thom down in some leaves, and went to the riverside and took Yaw's knife from her belt. She remembered it was to have been a gift for Adou, and she held it a moment, thinking about what she had lost. Then, gritting her teeth, Nanny dug out the English bullet that had settled deep into her flesh.

She washed the wound with the fresh river water and bound her shoulder with her headwrap. It hurt, but not as much as the loss of Adou. And of her people. Her warriors. Her family.

When she returned to the tree, Thom was awake, and although he cried for his mother, Nanny lifted him onto her hip and began to walk.

She walked back into town, thinking there might be some things – pots, pans, spades, tools, even blankets – that could be saved.

The dead were too many to bury or burn. No one could live here any more. There was blood soaked into the soil where they used to dance. The gardens were trampled, most of the huts burnt or smashed by cannon.

She picked up a spade, perhaps one that Adou had used on the tree trunk that had ruined her garden, and she stopped, leaned on it, and thought about how much time had been wasted, how many lives destroyed. Her throat felt dry. For a moment she could not move for the great weight of sadness. Then there was a shout from the forest and Quao, Kofi, Hester and some of her warriors burst out of the bush, Michele trotting along at their side. Their faces told her they carried that sadness too.

After they had done their best for the dead and sung a song for their spirits, they talked.

'They take some of them alive,' Quao said. 'I see them marched down to Port Antonio, chained together. They taking them back to they masters no doubt.'

Kofi closed his eyes as Nanny thought that at least Adou would never be captive again. He had died a free man. A small small blessing.

Nanny made a fire close to the Cattawood spring, away from the town, and they salvaged what they could from the gardens. She boiled up some healing herbs and made poultices for those who needed them. There was only about a quarter of the townsfolk left. Quite a few had deep wounds from swords or lances or bullets, and she washed and bathed every one of their wounds. By nightfall she was exhausted.

Nanny could tell Quao wanted to talk to her; he kept trying to catch her eye and she could feel the anger that seemed to come off him as if every look hurled daggers.

When everyone else was asleep he confronted her.

'We move in the morning,' Quao said. 'At first light.'

Nanny looked at him. She still felt as if the sound of the explosions was singing in her brain. 'What?'

'West to Accompong Town, to Cudjoe's people. We can't stay, you must see that.'

Nanny said nothing for a long moment. The fire spat and crackled. All around her people slept on the ground. Up in the sky the stars were like spilt milk on a black cloth.

A night bird called from away in the bush, and both she and Quao jumped a little.

'We can't stay. Not after this massacre,' Quao said again. 'You may have lost Adou—'

Nanny interrupted. 'Not only Adou. We have all lost. We have lost our town and ourselves.'

'You are not our leader any more,' Quao said. He did not look at her, but into the moving flames. His face was blank, the look in his eyes just as damaged and hurt as some of the worst wounded. 'Nanny Town is not a place now,' he said. He looked at her shoulder, where it was bandaged and where the blood was beginning to seep through. 'You could not save us this time.'

Nanny stood up, standing as tall as she could, even though her shoulder ached and throbbed.

'Nanny Town always a place,' she said. 'Even if the redcoats smoke us out, we still live, we still free. You go west if you feel to. You join with Cudjoe. Even when you do that, you still be Nanny Town people.'

'You're not coming?' Quao said. 'The English—'

'The English always come. And I will fight them on home ground. I say as we free we let people choose,' Nanny said. 'Those who want, go with you. Others can stay. We will build a new town, somewhere better. Better hidden.'

Quao kissed his teeth, then took out a blanket he had saved from one of the roofless huts and lay down to sleep.

Nanny put another piece of wood on the fire and hummed an old, old song from the other side of the ocean: one she hadn't known she remembered. She wondered if a time would come when she ever slept again.

When it was light she went out for a walk around the boundary of the old town. She found what was left of her old hut, the one she would have shared with Adou if they had married. She stepped inside and looked straight up at the sky. The clouds were heavy and grey. There would be more rain soon.

Then she went out into her garden. The pumpkins were smashed to pieces, and the callaloo was trampled down, but she collected some seeds as best she could, wrapping them in twists of cloth. She took seeds of the bolted sorrel flowers and some of the yam seedlings as well, those that weren't completely ruined.

Quao left in the morning, as he had said, and some of the others went with him.

A few others came with her east, carving out trails in the bush with cutlass and machete, up into the highest mountain. Atlas, Hester Jane and Kofi were among them, and Nanny brought little Thom.

They made a clearing close to where a spring bubbled up, and made shelters out of leaves and vines. But when Nanny looked for her bag of seeds and plants she found it was gone. Somewhere, back in the bush on the long climb up into the mountains, the seeds had all been lost. With a feeling like a sudden cold wind, Nanny remembered Meggy's message from Ophelia. Some seeds or somesuch. Ophelia had known. She had warned her, and Nanny had forgotten.

She steeled herself. They would have to make do with what they could. The seeds would have helped.

But she had survived with nothing before. She would do it again.

On the morning of the eighth day that they had made camp, Nanny was working at clearing some ground for a new garden when a bird flew up out of the bush – a storm crow calling, signalling rain – and then Michele came hurtling out of the undergrowth. The pig ran to Nanny and put her head down for her neck to be scratched. Nanny smiled, and she thought that was the first time she had smiled since the massacre.

Months passed. The ground was stony, and slow to clear and till. There were no cows or goats or chickens. A few wild guinea fowl came out of the bush, but they were hard to catch. They were higher up in the mountains now, and the trees that had dropped coconut and soursop, plantain and banana into their laps in the lower slopes seemed a long, long way away. A plague of insects finished off the sorrel and the callaloo before it could be harvested. Even the bush, which was usually so bountiful, seemed to have turned its back on Nanny and her people.

Nanny thought about walking down the mountain to see Ophelia. She wished for the old woman's counsel more than anything. Some days she felt so tired. Some days she thought perhaps Quao had been right, and they should all have travelled west.

She could see the children's bones under their skin, and their hard-swelling, empty bellies. She knew that Thom and some of the others would die if she didn't do something. Even big Atlas looked weak.

'We must kill that pig,' said Hester Jane. 'She got enough meat on her to feed the children. We got no choice.'

'That pig been with us a long time,' Nanny said, but she knew Hester Jane was right. Slaughtering Michele would give them time until there was fruit and callaloo, yam and mango.

That night Nanny lay on the ground looking up at the stars. She thought about what Ophelia would do, and about the power that she had felt – it all seemed so long ago. She put her palms flat down on the earth and sang. She sang to the spirit of the place and to the oldest gods she knew. She sang all the songs she could remember, the ones that had brought her to this island in sorrow and the ones that had delivered her through massacres, ambushes and death. Nanny sang to Yaw and Adou and to all her ancestors, here on the island and back across the sea on the Coromantee coast. She opened her heart and her mind, and hoped the stars were listening.

In the morning Nanny woke to find Hester Jane dressed and ready, knife out. 'Where is the pig? I look for her all over. We need her.'

Nanny nodded. There was no more argument. That pig would save the lives of her people.

'I haven't seen Michele since the last new moon,' Nanny said. 'But I promise I will look for her.'

'That animal!' Hester said.

'She is not stupid,' Nanny said. 'Even though she look so...'

'We need to eat, Nanny. Thom and all the others. Maybe it would have been better if the English kill us all...'

Nanny held Hester in a hug then. 'It will be all right,' she said. 'I will make it right.'

Nanny went into the bush to look for Michele. She trod softly as she made her way through the trees and the vines. Perhaps there would be a wild boar or some mountain doves, and she could let Michele live? It was foolish, she knew, but after everything she had lost, if she could spare this pig...

The sun was high, and even though the light trickled down through the leaf canopy in drops and moving puddles of green, Nanny felt hot and slow. She softly sang to herself, an old song, and tried to keep moving through the undergrowth. The light made everything move, green and gold and then black in the dark shade. Then suddenly Nanny saw a woman walking ahead – a long white dress, a headwrap of the same colour. It couldn't be...

'Ophelia?' Nanny spoke the word as a whisper. 'Ophelia...'

The woman turned, her shape dissolving and reforming in the dappled light. All at once there, and then not there; then there again.

Nanny gasped. She felt her breath catch. She knew then Ophelia was dead.

Her heart swooped and turned as Ophelia – what had been Ophelia – led her into a clearing.

The light danced on the open ground, green and gold again, and Ophelia was gone. Nanny could feel her heart galloping under her ribs, overcome by a wave of sadness and joy. She looked up to the open sky, and knew her old friend was at peace.

Nanny steadied herself against the trunk of a tree. She had a sudden feeling that somehow, everything would be all right.

A snuffling snorting sound, like a small baby, drew her back to here and now. She looked, to see five piglets, spotted and striped like the wild boar, all feeding from Michele as the pig lay back, trotters up, in a hollow on the far side of the clearing. Nanny would swear that she was smiling.

Ophelia had led her to Michele. To what she had been seeking. Nanny raised her gun, apologized to the spirit of the animal, and to Yaw – and then she felt something. A cool cool breeze like a hand on her forehead.

Nanny felt her finger on the trigger relax. 'Ophelia?' There was a sound in the breeze, wasn't there? Nanny put the gun down. Listened hard to the wind, and to her heart, and the sound of Michele feeding her happy, healthy babies.

This was a sign. How could she kill Michele when clearly her babies would provide, in time, more food, more life?

Nanny shut her eyes. But if she didn't take this life, what would her people eat? When she opened them again she saw something caught on a bush at the side of the clearing. A cloth bag. *Her* cloth bag! The one she had lost! Nanny tucked her gun into her belt and went to look. It was!

She opened it and there were the yam seedlings – still alive, root and tip. There were the callaloo seeds, and there, more than a dozen dozen handfuls of pumpkin seeds.

Nanny let Michele be. Told her to come back to town and give one of her children soon for her warriors. In the meantime she took the bag back to camp.

Hester Jane had already built a fire. Nanny had thought about how she would talk Hester round; after all, pumpkin seeds were no match for jerk pork.

But Hester was smiling too. 'See, Nanny!' She held up two pairs of guinea fowl. 'Kofi and the children catch these fine birds!'

'Someone watching over Kofi and the children too,' said Nanny, and she told the others about Michele, and Ophelia.

'*Medaase*,' said Kofi. 'I think Adou still with us.'

Nanny felt tears come to her eyes for the first time in months. But she was smiling. 'I think so too,' she said.

And then they roasted the pumpkin seeds, and everyone feasted.

The day after, Nanny opened the bag, thinking to plant the yam seedlings and the callaloo seeds, and was surprised to find there were still some pumpkin seeds left in the bag too. Hadn't she roasted all of them last night?

Or had Ophelia made sure she had missed some?

She decided to plant them with the yam and the callaloo.

And the plants grew sturdy and green, and her people had enough to eat until the storm crows called for the next rains.

PEACE

Nanny was pounding cassava with Hester Jane, taking turns to pound the root with a pestle to soften it for flour, when Quao and his party came out of the trees. Every one of them looked worn and tired and thin, and at first she didn't recognize them. Even Quao's red coat flapped large on his bony body.

All at once she handed the pestle to Hester and wiped her hands on her apron.

'Thom, set the fire – now – and fetch some water.' Nanny put her people to work preparing food and drink.

Quao sat down by the fire, all bone-deep exhaustion. Nanny handed him a cup of ginger tea and he took it gratefully.

'We get to Accompong all right,' he said, and shook his head. 'We walk for months, but we do find it. Then it turn out Cudjoe sign some treaty with that Governor Gregory.'

'A treaty?' said Nanny. 'With the English?'

Quao nodded. 'The English leave them alone, but in exchange, if any escaped slaves come to them, they send them back to their masters.'

The thought made Nanny's blood run cold.

'Governor Gregory and his people, he talked to me. He said he make the same treaty with us.' Quao looked at his warriors and they nodded. 'With you.'

Nanny kissed her teeth, leaned back and shook her head. 'Never. Send people back to them? People just like us, looking for freedom? Even if we agree to that – you really trust them?' she said. 'After everything they do?' She got up and walked away from the fireside to her hut. 'May as well trust red ant not to bite!' she called.

The moon changed once, twice, running through her shapes as the year turned, but Quao would not give up. He was sure a treaty like Cudjoe's would keep them safe. At the coming of the third moon, he disappeared in the forest and returned, sounding his abeng and walking into town with a redcoat.

Nanny felt the island's anger through every bone

in her body. She took Quao aside and spoke to him as sharply as she ever could.

'These men kill us and you bring them here!'

Quao was adamant. 'We need peace, Nanny! We need to grow food and feed children. We need to stop war.'

Nanny could not look at him. She walked out of town into the bush. She found the clearing where she had seen Ophelia and hoped the old woman would appear again. But she did not.

She knew there was something in what Quao said. The English would not stop. This way Nanny Town could flourish and grow without the constant, aching threat of fire or cannon or dog or starvation. Of massacre and destruction.

But how could she agree to cooperate with people who thought they were no better than property? How could she send people who thought they had found freedom back into captivity?

It was Kofi who persuaded her in the end.

'You know, we all escaped slaves,' he said one night. 'Only difference is time. They not respect us – why should we respect them? Say we sign the treaty. Say someone escape. Find his way here. We hide him long enough, they really going to remember his face when they not looking for him any more?'

Nanny hummed. There was something to what Kofi said. 'Perhaps you right,' she said. 'Perhaps that way we even help more people.'

She mulled it over for a week before she decided to let Quao do it. Governor Gregory promised her people one thousand acres, but – trust? And surely surely, when Quao signed the treaty, they had changed their mind. It would only be five hundred acres.

Nanny laughed when he told her. 'And they expect us to send every runaway we find to them?'

'Is better than nothing, Nanny,' said Quao.

'True true,' said Nanny.

And it was.

And even though she was elderly and her joints were painful, Nanny would walk the forest, sometimes with one of Michele's daughters at her side, and if she found a runaway, hotfoot for freedom, she would take them in. Hide them till they just another one of her people.

Nanny was lying on her bed when Ophelia came again to see her, this time with Yaw. She looked up and there in the doorway of the hut was Adou too.

But it was Quao who spoke. 'Nanny?' he said. 'Nanny, I know we don't see eye to eye always…' His eyes were shining, damp.

'You my best warrior,' she said.

Yaw sat down cross-legged on the floor.

'I will miss you, Nanny,' Quao said. 'You like our mother.'

'I always look after my people,' Nanny said, only her voice was small and sounded far away. 'I will be back. You'll see, every year. Every year.'

'Nanny,' Adou said… and came towards her and took her hand.

'Adou,' she said, and part of her sat up and swung her legs out of bed. She felt no pain in her joints any more, and she felt light and free and she walked with Adou and Ophelia and Yaw out of her hut, and stepped up into the blue, shining sky.

And flew all the way home.

A LITTLE MORE ABOUT
QUEEN NANNY

A REAL WOMAN

Queen Nanny of the Maroons was a real woman. She lived sometime in the early part of the 18th century. She was a Coromantee, probably from what is Ghana today. There are many tales of Nanny's exploits; she was a renowned guerrilla fighter, she set traps and ambushes for the redcoats. Perhaps because she was successful the British could not imagine that she could win without magic – Obeah. Although there is so much written about her as an Obeah woman, I think there is definitely some truth in her skills as a tactical fighter, and her charisma.

It is not known how or exactly when Nanny came to Jamaica; it is said she was never enslaved and was always free.

And it has been hard to write about her, as so little is known for certain, and history is always written by the victors, in this case the English.

In Jamaica today, both Maroon towns still exist – Accompong, home of the Leeward Maroons who were led by Cudjoe, and the Windward Maroons in New Nanny Town, which the British referred to as Moore Town from 1760.

Although some of the people in this story were real – Captain Shettlewood, Quao, Cudjoe – I have made up many others. I've had to fill in the gaps as Nanny is truly, and in the most literal way, legendary.

Nanny probably died sometime in the 1750s, but it's not known for certain. Some sources say she died later between 1760 and 1770. She is said to be buried at a spot called Bump Grave.

She was declared a National Hero in Jamaica in 1976, her portrait features on the 500-dollar note, and there is more than one memorial to her on the island.

The British never managed to destroy Maroon society, and after more conflict and more treaties the Maroons were eventually left alone. The towns of Accompong and Moore Town had their own laws and operated outside of colonial government. When Jamaica gained its independence in 1962, the rights and customs of the Maroon areas in the mountains were protected.

It's also said that every year, on the day of her death at a special ceremony in Moore Town, Nanny's ghost appears to make sure her people are safe.

OBEAH

Obeah is one of the religions and systems of belief and healing that crossed the Atlantic with the enslaved peoples of West Africa. It originated in what we call Ghana today. Laws were passed to forbid its practice in Jamaica in the 1760s after several important slave rebellions, including Tacky's war, an uprising that terrified the English colonists.

Part of Nanny's legend was that she was a gifted Obeah woman who could harness magic and spirits and catch bullets. There were so many stories about her that the British were terrified of the idea of her. Of course, Nanny made use of this – a terrified enemy was easier to overcome.

TIMELINE

1494 Christopher Columbus claims Jamaica for Spain.

1655 The British defeat the Spanish, take control of Jamaica and begin to develop sugar plantations worked by large numbers of slaves.

1655 and after Escaped slaves, originally brought to the island from West Africa by the Spanish but later by the British, set up communities in the Windward area of the Blue Mountains. They are known as the Maroons.

1673 Other Maroons establish communities in the Leeward area of the Blue Mountains.

1674–1683 Welshman and pirate Captain Harry Morgan serves as Governor of Jamaica, leading several unsuccessful expeditions to defeat the Maroons.

c. 1686 Nanny born to the Ashanti people of Ghana, in West Africa.

1728 Major-General Robert Hunter becomes Governor of Jamaica. He launches attacks against the Windward Maroons; the First Maroon War begins.

1729–1737 Varied fighting between the English and the two Maroon communities.

The Leeward Maroons assault the north-east town of Port Antonio and defeat British forces sent after them.

The Windward Maroons, led by Nanny, inflict a heavy defeat on British forces who come to attack them.

This is followed by many successful defences, organized by Nanny, of Nanny Town against smaller groups of English soldiers, and attacks on slave-owning planters.

Under new Governor John Gregory, the English finally attack and destroy Nanny Town with the help of the 'Black Shot' militia and the Meskito.

The Maroons retreat further into the Blue Mountains.

1738 Edward Trelawny appointed Governor. Deciding that the British cannot defeat the Maroons, he offers peace terms.

1739 Peace treaty signed with Cudjoe of the Leeward Maroons.

20th April 1740 Peace treaty signed with Nanny of the Windward Maroons.

Over thirty years Nanny is credited with freeing more than 1000 slaves. In Moore Town – as Nanny Town was renamed – 20th April is celebrated each year as a holiday. Her image is on the $500 Jamaican bill, which is known as a 'Nanny'.

GLOSSARY

ABENG   musical instrument made from an animal's horn, used to communicate over long distances.

BUCKRA   white man.

CALLALOO   vegetable dish, the main ingredient of which is the leaf of the amaranth plant.

CASSAVA   shrub with starchy roots, from which a sort of porridge (tapioca) can be made.

CHIGGERS   tiny parasites (like ticks) that attach themselves to animals or people and feed on their skin, causing swelling and irritation.

COFFLE   line of animals or slaves fastened together.

COROMANTEES   people from the area known today as Ghana, in West Africa.

CUSTARD APPLE   yellow-brown fruit with a sweet taste like custard.

DUPPY   ghost or spirit.

GRIS GRIS   amulet (piece of jewellery or an ornament, such as a bracelet or necklace) believed to keep the wearer safe from evil.

GUINEP   tree bearing small green fruit with a bitter-sweet flavour.

GUNGO PEAS   green or purple peas of the gungo tree.

HOG-APPLE TREE   tree bearing a foul-smelling, bitter fruit, pale yellow in colour when ripe.

MASSA   dialect word for 'master', in other words the slave-owners and overseers.

MEDAASE   'thank you' in the Twi language of Ghana, in West Africa.

MEROE TREE   blue mahoe tree, national tree of Jamaica, which has blue-green streaks in its bark.

OBEAH   folk religion of spiritual and healing practices found throughout the Caribbean but originating in Nigeria, in West Africa.

PAWPAW   edible fruit of the asimina tree, yellowish brown when ripe, tasting a little like banana, and a little like mango.

PLANTAIN   banana-like fruit usually cooked before being eaten.

SHAMEY PLANT   mimosa plant, often used to cure ailments.

SORREL   herb with edible sour-tasting leaves.

SOURSOP TREE   evergreen tree with prickly green fruit, smelling of pineapple, tasting like strawberries and apple.

YAMS   edible tubers, like sweet potatoes.

TRUE ADVENTURES

INCREDIBLE PEOPLE
DOING INCREDIBLE THINGS

The most thrilling stories in history

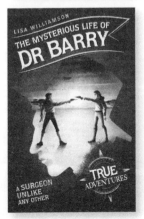

NAZI GERMANY, 1942

As World War Two rages, Sophie Scholl reunites with her beloved brother Hans in Munich. Soon she meets his young student friends. Like her they can take no more of the war.

Then leaflets calling for a revolt against Hitler start appearing, put out by a mysterious group called the White Rose. Who are these people? No one knows. But the Gestapo is determined to hunt them down – and suddenly Sophie finds herself in the most terrible danger.

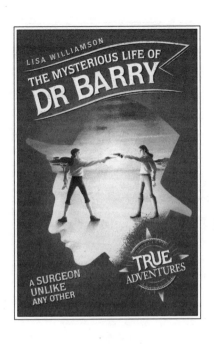

SOUTH AFRICA, 1808

Dr James Barry was Inspector General of Hospitals at the height of the British Empire, one of the most distinguished surgeons of his day, famous for his brilliance. In South Africa he carried out one of the world's first Caesarean operations in which both mother and child survived. He was also famous for his severity and prickly temper: when young he fought a duel and, in the Crimea, publicly delivered a rebuke to Florence Nightingale for lack of hygiene. Yet when his dead body was laid out an incredible secret was discovered about him.

ANCIENT CHINA, THE YEAR 1000

It began with a duel. When General Yang wanted to get rid of a troublesome bandit, he sent his fiercest warrior: his son, Captain Zongbao. But on his way through the forest to find the outlaw, Zongbao unexpectedly encountered the bandit's teenage daughter, Mu Guiying – who challenged him to unarmed combat. And she was better.

The fight launched Mu Guiying's astonishing journey from fearless outcast to the great defender of her country, as she masterminded the Chinese defence against the invading horsemen from the north.